Carey Miller

Baffling mysteries

A collection of weird problems and unsolved riddles

cover illustration by Richard Hook
text illustrations by Angelo Cinque

A Piccolo Original Pan Books

To David – for paying my library fines

Also by Carey Miller in Piccolo

A Dictionary of Monsters and Mysterious Beasts
Airships and Balloons
Submarines!

First published 1976 by Pan Books Ltd,
Cavaye Place, London SW10 9PG

ISBN 0 330 24677 1
Printed and bound in Great Britain by
Richard Clay (The Chaucer Press) Ltd, Bungay, Suffolk

Contents

1 The strange hoofmarks of the Devonshire Devil 5
2 *Waratah:* the ship that vanished 12
3 The secret of the Eilean Mor light 19
4 The flaming cross 26
5 The riddle of the Oak Island money pit 32
6 The creeping coffins of Barbados 39
7 The incredible affair of the dancing furniture 47
8 The elusive monster of Loch Ness 53
9 Flight into the unknown 60
10 The riddle of the *Mary Celeste* 66
11 Borley Rectory: the most haunted house in England 71
12 Orffyreus and his wheel of eternity 78
13 The Russian princess: alive or dead? 84
14 The strange curse of the Lost Dutchman's Mine 92

Introduction

Everybody loves a mystery, whether it is woven around the clever, old-fashioned detective work of Sherlock Holmes or the more up-to-date excitement of a James Bond thriller with its twists of plot and space-age technology. We all breathe a sigh of relief at the end of the final chapter when the clues are gathered together, the pieces fall into place like a jigsaw puzzle, and we finally discover who did what to whom and why.

The unsolved mysteries of the past have no such neat endings, but they have real beginnings and involve real people. Maybe this is what makes them all the stranger and more difficult to fathom. Certainly they make exciting reading!

This book is a collection of mysteries which have occurred during the last three hundred years, each one of which aroused a great deal of interest and speculation in its time. Although a thorough investigation took place in each case, none of them was ever satisfactorily solved. These tales of mystery have certainly puzzled me, and if any young readers can help me to unravel any of the knots I should be delighted to hear from them!

1 The strange hoofmarks of the Devonshire Devil

One snowy night in February 1855 the county of Devon was visited by an uncanny animal with hoofs like a donkey's. Yet this donkey could walk upright like a man and cover a hundred miles in a single night! This was no donkey, said the people of Devon, but the Devil himself! *The Times*, a sober and respectable newspaper, printed the following report:

EXTRAORDINARY OCCURRENCE

Considerable sensation has been evoked in the towns of Topsham, Lympstone, Exmouth, Teignmouth and Dawlish, in the south of Devon, in consequence of the discovery of a vast number of foot tracks of a most strange and mysterious description. The superstitious go so far as to believe that they are the marks of Satan himself; and that great excitement has been produced among all classes may be judged from the fact that the subject has been descanted from the pulpit. It appears that on Thursday night last there was a heavy fall of snow in the neighbourhood of Exeter and South Devon. On the following morning the inhabitants of the above towns were surprised at discovering the tracks of some strange and mysterious animal, endowed with the power of ubiquity, as the footprints were to be seen in all kinds of inaccessible places – on the tops of houses and narrow walls, in gardens and courtyards enclosed by high walls and palings, as well as open fields. There was hardly a garden in Lympstone where the footprints were not observed.

The track appeared more like that of a biped rather than a quadruped and the steps were generally eight inches in advance of each other. The impressions of the feet closely resembled that of a donkey's shoe and measured from an inch and a half (in some instances) to two and a half inches across. Here and there it appeared as if cloven, but in the generality of the steps the shoe was continuous, and, from the snow in the centre remaining entire, merely showing the outer crest of the foot, it must have been convex.

The creature seems to have approached the doors of several houses and then to have retreated, but no one has been able to discover the standing or resting point of this mysterious visitor. On Sunday last the Rev Mr Musgrave alluded to the subject in his sermon and suggested the possibility of the footprints being those of a kangaroo, but this could scarcely have been the case as they were found on both sides of the estuary of the Exe.

At present it remains a mystery, and many superstitious people in the above towns are actually afraid to go outside their doors after night.

*

This remarkable piece of news caused curiosity and excitement all over the country but in Devon it also brought fear! It happened at a time when the British were heavily involved in the Crimean War. February was a particularly bad period for the British army whose numbers were being decimated by sickness and disease in faraway Russia. Naturally the newspapers were much more interested in serious news of their countrymen than in the nocturnal gallivantings of a donkey, even if it did turn out to be the Devil. *The Times* certainly had no more time to bother with the story, but the *Illustrated London News* was more curious and asked the Devonshire people to write in and give their accounts of what they had seen. They were quite unprepared for the avalanche of letters they received, and on February 24th and March 17th they printed as many of them as they had room for in their columns.

One 'on the spot' witness who signed himself 'South Devon' wrote a very long and interesting letter. He said:

The marks which appeared on the snow (which lay very thinly on the ground at the time), and which were seen on the Friday morning, to all appearance were the perfect impression of a donkey's hoof – the length four inches by two and three-quarter inches; but, instead of progressing as that animal would have done (or as any other animal would have done), feet right and left, it appeared that foot followed foot *in a single file*; the distance from each tread being eight inches, or rather more – the footmarks in each parish being exactly the same size and the steps the same length.

This mysterious visitor generally only passed once down or across each garden or courtyard, and did so in nearly all the houses in many parts of the several towns above mentioned, as also in the farms scattered about; this regular track passing in some instances over the roofs of the houses and haystacks, and very high walls (one fourteen feet), without displacing the snow on either side or alternating the distance between the feet, and passing on as if the wall had not been any impediment. The gardens with high fences or walls, and gates locked, were equally visited as those open and unprotected!

*

Obviously there were no barriers that could keep this weird creature out! Someone wrote to say that in his village the animal had entered a shed and emerged at the back through a hole only six inches across; another person wrote to say that where he lived the creature had crawled through a narrow drainpipe, leaving its tracks at either end! All the letters reported the hoofprints climbing haystacks and crossing streams and wide rivers. The most amazing thing, of course, was the mileage that these odd hoofs appeared to have covered in the space of just one night. The hoofmarks started at Exmouth, crossed a two-mile stretch of the river Exe and finished at Totnes – or vice versa. Taking into account the trips through people's gardens, on to their doorsteps, through haystacks and over the roofs of houses, the creature must have covered a distance of at least a hundred miles and all without a single eye-witness! On the whole of the trail there seemed to be no place where the mysterious stranger had stopped or rested. It just seemed to have landed in one place, trundled along with a machine-like rhythm and then disappeared into thin air.

Another thing that distressed the local people was the unusual clarity of the hoofprints. One correspondent said that the prints appeared to have been cut with a diamond or branded with a hot iron, whereas the fresh tracks of cats, dogs, other animals and birds found on the same morning were less distinct and had a completely different look about them. Finally Sir Richard Owen, the famous naturalist of the period, made an announcement. He said that the prints could only have been made by a badger. He explained that it was the only plantigrade (an animal which places the whole sole of the foot on the ground when walking) quadruped in Britain. It places its back feet in such a way that it gives the impression of walking in a line of single steps. As it is an animal that sleeps a lot in winter, but doesn't hibernate completely, it does occasionally come out to forage for food

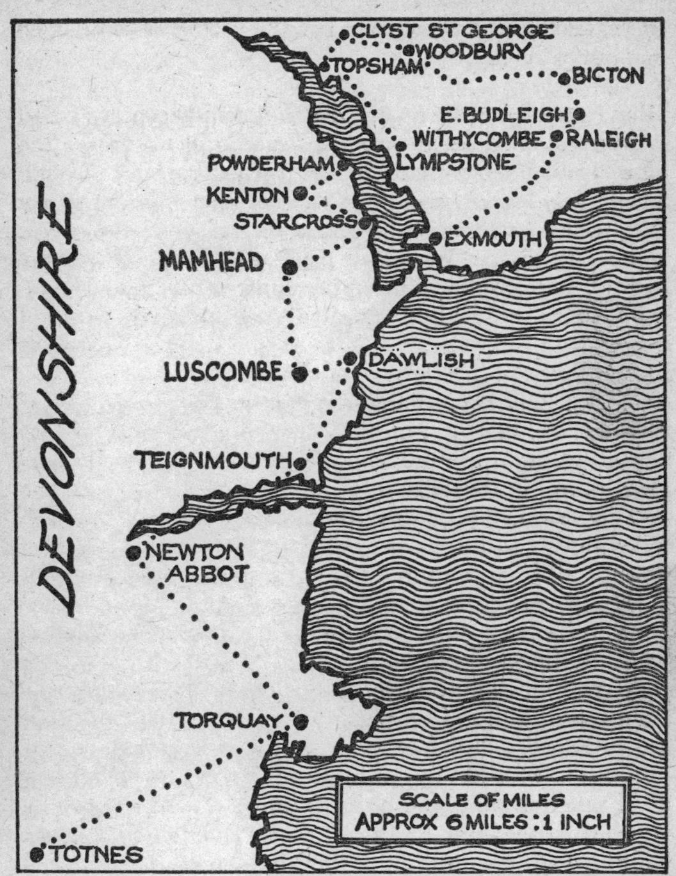

The hoofmarks were seen in all these towns and villages. The dotted line shows the shortest distance a single creature would have to have travelled in order to visit them all

when the weather is bad. It does seem rather unlikely, though, that one badger could forage for a hundred miles without stopping, however hungry he might have been at the time. In any case, badgers don't normally jump over haystacks or swim two-mile rivers at a stretch!

Another man, Thomas Fox, suggested that the marks could have been made by all four feet of a leaping rat. It would have to have been a clever rat to jump exactly 8½ inches every time, except, of course, when it leapt over the Exe estuary – rather a longer jump! After this, explanations were offered involving half the British animal kingdom. Some people favoured birds and suggested that the marks had been made by turkeys, moorhens, swans and even sea-gulls; others scorned the bird theories and insisted that the marks had been made by otters, polecats, rabbits, hares, frogs, in fact just about everything except cats and dogs! The suggestion that the prints had been made by one of the kangaroos from a private zoo at Sidmouth was soon disregarded when it was discovered that the kangaroos in question had never left the safety of their cages!

The local country people steadfastly rejected all these explanations: this was Satan's work, they whispered. The Devil had visited Devon to remind them of his evil presence. Another letter from Devon tells us of 'aged crones and trembling old men' who refused to stir out of doors after sunset. Even the children, apparently, huddled around their firesides, frightened by the rumours of rampaging monsters. In one district the local shopkeepers, armed with guns and sticks, formed a search party to track the 'evil one' to his lair, but as far as we know they never found him. Even the local clergymen pleaded with their congregations to throw off their evil ways and repent before it was too late. The Devil had given his warning! A Polish doctor, then resident in Heidelberg, wrote to tell the readers of the *Illustrated London News* that on a small hill in Galacia such marks are to be seen every winter and the local people always attribute them to the Devil as no other explanation for them has ever been found.

At that time, over 120 years ago, the supernatural explanation was usually preferred because most people, especially the ones who lived in the more remote parts of the country, were still very superstitious. One thing is certain, whatever the footprints were really like they were certainly terrifyingly unusual as country folk are familiar with animal tracks of all kinds. These footmarks must have been very different to throw them into such a panic, and there is no doubt that hundreds of people really did see the prints.

Even if the number of miles the animal covered had been exaggerated, it would still be impossible for a medium-sized animal to cover even fifty miles between the hours of dusk and dawn, including haystacks and the roofs of houses. As far as we know, the mysterious hoofprints have not been seen in Devon, or any other part of Britain, since that day, so we have had no further opportunity to discover the creature's true identity!

2 *Waratah:* the ship that vanished

The sea has always been a great keeper of secrets, and the number of people and ships that have disappeared into it without trace would fill the pages of a very large book. Enormous modern ships equipped with first-class radio apparatus have vanished for ever on calm, sunny seas even though rescue ships and planes have raked thousands of miles of ocean and found no trace of their passing. The watery fate of the steamship *Waratah* was not as mysterious as that of other ships, for doubts about her stability were voiced from the captain down to the stewards. Nevertheless, her strange disappearance was so accurately described in advance by one of her passengers that the *Waratah*'s loss makes a very curious story indeed!

The steamship *Waratah* was launched at Clydebank in 1908; she was a twin-screwed vessel of 16,800 tons with three decks fore and aft, and was considered the most modern cargo-passenger vessel ever built. Yet in spite of many refinements for the amusement and comfort of her passengers, she had no radio equipment. Blue Anchor, the owners, had their inspectors check her, the Board of Trade inspectors checked her, Lloyd's the insurance people checked her and so did the experts at the Immigration Authority. In fact, no ship had ever been examined by so many experts and it was a great triumph for the builders when she was pronounced in 'A1' condition by all concerned.

The captaincy was given to Captain Ilbery, a sailor with forty years' experience, and under his command the ship sailed off to Australia and back on her maiden voyage. Immediately after docking, however, he complained to the owners about the *Waratah*'s lack of stability. He said that she could not be manoeuvred in dock unless she was weighted down with ballast, a curious thing to have to do with a brand-new ship! The owners sent the captain's report to the builders, who were openly disbelieving and rather insulted! Blue Anchor, satisfied by the builders' convincing arguments, treated the lack of stability as a figment of Captain Ilbery's imagination and the whole matter was dropped. On 27 April 1909 the *Waratah* once more set out for Australia, a voyage which apparently went off without mishap. Two months later, on July 7th, she left Adelaide for the voyage back to London via Durban and Cape Town. Up to now weather conditions had been very favourable for the new steamship, but on the fourth day out the winds began to strengthen and the seas became grey and angry. Even though these were hardly storm conditions, one person, a young Englishman named Claude Sawyer, was far from happy. He had been approached by a kindly older passenger, an Australian solicitor called Ebsworth, who thought the youth was seasick. Sawyer explained that he did not feel sick so much as terrified by what he thought was the *Waratah*'s abnormal rolling and shuddering. Ebsworth was surprised to see such fear in the young man's eyes and thought he must be a very nervous passenger to get himself into such an anxious state. Sawyer told Ebsworth that although this was only his second sea trip, he thought that the new steamship was coping very badly with weather conditions which could not really be classed as rough. Something about Sawyer's extreme fear caught hold of Ebsworth and he suddenly began to notice just how violently the ship was pitching. He suggested to Sawyer that they should go up to the front of the boat and observe the ship's behaviour from there. As they stood in the bows Ebsworth was horrified to see just how heavy the great ship seemed and how difficult she found it to rise from the trough of each wave. More often than not she was unable to breast the waves at all and plunged right through them, sending sheets of water over the decks. And all the time the two men could feel that ominous and persistent shudder! Ebsworth now became convinced that things were not as they should be, so together the two went to see the Captain. The Captain was not available at that time, but they were told that he would be pleased to speak with them in the saloon after dinner that evening.

The ship's commander appeared at the appointed time, smiling and unruffled, and asked how he could help them. Sawyer, flushed and embarrassed, told the Captain that he thought the ship was top-heavy, dangerously sluggish and seemed to list to starboard.

'Whenever I have a bath,' he said, 'the bath water lists at an angle of forty-five degrees – surely that can't be right!'

The Captain frowned. 'I must admit,' he said, 'this ship is certainly not as steady as my last one and she does have a tendency to roll rather more than I'm used to, but I can assure you that she really is an excellent ship, strong, well designed and very seaworthy. You can put any ideas of her being dangerous right out of your head!'

The Captain smiled rather less warmly than before and excused himself, leaving Sawyer and Ebsworth feeling foolish but certainly reassured. Their relief was to be short-lived, however.

A few minutes later Ebsworth fell into conversation with a steward who, flung across the gangway by one of the steamship's more spectacular rolls, had dropped and broken some empty glasses. When Ebsworth showed concern, the steward told him of the amazing number of crockery breakages that had taken place on the ship since she left London. Sawyer and Ebsworth pricked up their ears and Sawyer, beginning to feel nervous all over again, asked the steward what he thought about the *Waratah*'s violent behaviour.

The steward turned white and glanced nervously over his shoulder. 'If you really want to know, sir, I'm very frightened. The crockery is nothing compared with some of the things that are breaking up aboard this ship!'

'What do you mean?' gasped Sawyer hoarsely, his hands beginning to tremble again.

'Well,' said the steward, 'it's the whole of the promenade deck, it's breaking loose from its beams. The bolts that hold it down are nearly all broken. One fell on to the baker's head this morning!'

Ebsworth and Sawyer stared at each other in dismay. This was even worse than they had imagined.

'If you really want my opinion,' went on the steward, 'this ship is going to make a very big hole in the water one day. Some of the crew are already calling it a floating coffin!' He then scuffled off, leaving Sawyer and Ebsworth feeling worse than they had felt before the Captain's interview, and the two passengers spent an anxious and uneasy night. By the morning, however, the weather had changed dramatically and the *Waratah* was gliding over seas now as smooth as glass. Day after day the great steamship surged happily along without a single shudder or vibration of any kind. Ebsworth soon forgot that he had ever been scared and even Sawyer calmed down and almost began to enjoy the voyage.

All went smoothly until the night of July 28th when Claude Sawyer interrupted the slumbers of his fellow passengers with the most terrifying screams they had ever heard. Apparently he had been having a nightmare of such intensity that even after he awoke he was still in a state of severe shock. The ship's doctor was called and said that Sawyer gave the impression of having survived some terrible experience. Sawyer seemed very shaken after the dream and told the other passengers that it had been a warning to him to get off the ship. In his dream a strangely dressed man had appeared, held a sword over Sawyer's head and then showed him his other hand which was drenched with blood. When the blood started dripping on to Sawyer's face, he woke up and began to scream. In spite of the fact that the *Waratah* was still sailing serenely along in calm seas, Sawyer was determined to get off at the next port of call, even though it would cause him considerable extra expense and several days' delay. He was now even more anxious than he had been at the beginning of the trip and pleaded with Ebsworth and several other passengers to leave the ship. No one took him seriously, however, and most of the passengers were relieved when he disembarked at Durban after begging Ebsworth for the last time to accompany him. Sawyer immediately sent a telegram to his wife saying 'THOUGHT WARATAH TOP-HEAVY. LANDED DURBAN' and went to a hotel where he rested for two days. He then went along to the local office of the Union Castle Line to book passage on another ship.

As soon as he arrived at the office he insisted on seeing the manager and told him that, although it might involve him in a long wait, he wanted to travel on a really stable ship. As the manager found this request rather unusual, Sawyer went on to recount his fears for the safety of the *Waratah* and told the manager quite definitely that she would sink before reaching Cape Town. He then went back to his hotel and that night had another nightmare in which he saw the

Waratah ploughing through heavy seas. Suddenly a larger wave than the rest rolled her over on to her starboard side and she sank into the depths of the ocean. He awoke shaking and sobbing. That was on 27 July 1909.

Soon after dawn on the very same day the *Waratah* crept over the horizon. The seas were in an ugly mood that morning as she ploughed through them, but the ship was keeping up a good speed in spite of it as she passed the *Clan McIntyre*, a small steamer travelling on the same route. The tiny ship exchanged greetings with the large one by signal lamp and then the *Waratah*, having passed her, forged on purposefully round the Cape of Good Hope. The winds strengthened to gale force and the towering waves buffeted the little steamer as she surged on in the wake of the *Waratah*. The *Clan McIntyre* arrived at Cape Town without damage, as did ten other small ships which were in the area at the time. The Captain of the *Clan McIntyre* looked around the harbour and was surprised to find that the fast *Waratah* had not got there before his ship. He was quite sure that he could not have passed her without noticing. Other slower ships began to arrive, also using the same route from Durban, but none of them had seen a sign of her either. The steamship *Waratah* was now well overdue.

A search began which was to continue for many weeks. Three warships scoured the whole area, the Blue Anchor line chartered the *Sabine*, a fast ship, to search for the *Waratah*, and the Australian government commissioned the *Severn* to help her look. The *Sabine* searched without a break for nearly three months and covered 14,000 miles altogether. She found not the slightest trace of the *Waratah*, not a lifeboat or a lifebelt, not even a plank of wood. Nothing! The master of the *Tottenham*, another ship using the route, thought he had seen several bodies floating in the water. He turned his ship round to take a second look but all he could see were a lot of jellyfish and sunfish floating on top of the water.

It was a catastrophe that rocked the world and baffled the experts. How could a ship of nearly 17,000 tons with over a hundred people on board vanish without a trace! Where were all the deck fittings, the wooden deck-chairs, the lifeboats and all the hundreds of small things on board that always float above the graves of dead ships? Not to mention the hundred dead people! Newspapers put forward several spectacular theories, but it was soon decided that even the most violent explosion or the fastest-burning fire could not have destroyed a ship the size of the *Waratah* without leaving any evidence at all – especially on a busy shipping lane.

A Board of Trade inquiry opened in London in December 1910 and a row broke out which raged for two months. The ordinary seamen who had observed the *Waratah* in action soon after her launching said that she was hopelessly unseaworthy right from the start. The experts who had designed her insisted that she was as stable as a rock in any weather and in their opinion completely unsinkable – like the *Titanic*, for instance! Various stewards who had served on her and left before she vanished gave their accounts of her peculiar and violent behaviour at sea. The most sensational witness, of course, was Claude Sawyer, who told of his premonitions of disaster. His story was confirmed by witnesses from the Union Castle office, and the telegram he had sent his wife was shown in evidence.

As the inquiry continued it became obvious that no one was going to find any answer to the riddle of the *Waratah*. Finally the tragedy was declared to be 'an act of God', leaving the whole world still wondering how, when, where and why the *Waratah* had vanished. Probably she *was* thrown off her teetering balance at the wrong moment and tipped over in the same way that Sawyer imagined in his dream. Yet if that was the case, why was Sawyer singled out to receive the warning that was to save his life? Perhaps he was just a man with an overactive imagination who, by sheer fluke, happened to board an unseaworthy ship that was going to the bottom anyway. On the other hand, there are many unexplained things in this uncanny tale of a ship that vanished.

3 The secret of the Eilean Mor light

The Seven Hunters, or Flannan Islands, lie off the coast of Lewis in the Outer Hebrides in Scotland, and a place more wild and remote would be difficult to imagine. The islands themselves are little more than storm-swept rocks without a trace of land between them, and the coast of North America is thousands of miles away across the Atlantic. For centuries the people of the Hebrides have regarded the Seven Hunters as a very special place, possibly inhabited by fairies and kelpies (a sort of water-horse or monster), and even on the sunniest days sailors gave them a wide berth. On four of the islands there are small ruins dating from the eighth century, although the history of the people who built them is lost in the mists of time. In the seventeenth century St Flannan, the Bishop of Killaloe, built a small chapel on Eilean Mor, which is the largest of the seven islands, and lived there for several years with only the sea-birds for company. They were such good company, legend tells us, that they used to bring him fish in their beaks when the severe storms made it impossible for him to go fishing himself.

As far as we know, the Flannan Islands were not visited again until the hard times of the eighteenth century when some of the braver shepherds used to take their sheep over to the islands by the boatload so that they could graze on the Flannan turf. But however much the sheep enjoyed themselves, it is said that no man ever spent a night out there. Even if brilliant sunshine gave way to thick fog or howling blizzard, a shepherd would rather risk his life by returning home than stay on the Flannans after nightfall.

When Britain began to expand her sea trade in the 1890s many large merchant ships began to pass close by the Hebrides on their way to Scandinavian ports. In bad weather, which came often on this coast of Scotland, many of these ships found their way to the Seven Hunters and ended their days violently shattered on their rocks. So in 1895 the Northern Lighthouse Board decided to build a warning light on Eilean Mor. It was to be a 275-foot tower with a 140,000 candle-power light that would be visible for forty miles. It was to be sited near the ruins of St Flannan's chapel and was to have two landing stages – one to the east and one to the west, so that whichever way the wind was blowing there would be some shelter for the boats ferrying the lighthouse-keepers. The Eilean Mor light should have been finished easily in two years, but violent storms and malevolent winds caused the work to take twice as long and it was not finally completed until December 1899. Three lighthouse-keepers took up residence immediately and the light, which was to spell safety for all ships passing the Seven

Hunters, shone out boldly. But only for a year. In December 1900 the light went out and so began one of the weirdest riddles in the history of the sea.

Joseph Moore was one of a team of four lighthouse-keepers who worked the Eilean Mor light. The team worked on a rota system with three men always on the light and one man on leave. Joseph Moore had been unlucky enough to be allotted his leave time just before the Christmas period. He was luckier than he knew! Five nights before he was due to return for his Christmas stint he noticed with horror that there was complete blackness across the water. Although there was always the possibility of a complete mechanical breakdown, Moore had a dreadful premonition of disaster. He wanted to return to the lighthouse immediately, but gale-force winds made the crossing far too dangerous as it was unlikely that any steamer could avoid being thrown on the rocks and wrecked. Early on Boxing Day the gales died down and the Northern Light Board's steamer *Hesperus* took Moore, along with mail and Christmas presents for the other three keepers, over still-spiteful seas to the Flannan Islands. As they neared Eilean Mor the sky darkened ominously and the sea appeared to get even rougher. The captain of the *Hesperus* circled the island with extreme care and eventually landed at its eastern end. It took three attempts before the small steamer could be secured and her signals hoisted. The men in the lighthouse always signalled back with flags from the top window. They didn't on this day!

There had been no preparations for the boat's arrival, no empty provision boxes or mooring ropes on the jetty. Apart from the gulls' inhuman screeching, there seemed to be no life anywhere on the island. The silent men in the boat stared up at the tall tower and a cold shiver passed through them. All except Moore now felt a sudden reluctance to set foot on the island. Although thoroughly unnerved by the complete quiet, Moore was determined to discover the fate of his three friends. A rowboat was lowered from the side of the steamer and, after a long tussle with the tossing waves, it managed to draw in alongside the little jetty. Moore was out of the boat like a shot from a gun. He scrambled helter-skelter up the zig-zag steps and raced for the door of the lighthouse. It was firmly closed but not locked. Moore pulled it open and went inside.

There was the same uncanny stillness inside; the main rooms where the men ate were empty, yet clean and welcoming as if the inhabitants were due back at any moment. Now there was only the spiral staircase which led to the lantern. Here Moore's courage began to fail him. He shouted up the stairway again and again and desperately wanted to ascend, but he could not bring himself to begin the climb for fear of what horror he might find up there. He flung open the outer door and ran back to the boat. Two of the other seamen reluctantly agreed to come back with him, and together they went to investigate the top room of the lighthouse.

To their utter amazement it was quite deserted. There were no sick or dying men, as they had originally feared, but an emptiness so complete it was as if the three men had never existed at all. The men made a thorough search of the tower and then searched it all over again. They found not the slightest clue to the three men's disappearance, no signs of a struggle, no damage to the lighthouse, just freshly made beds, washed crockery and a well-maintained lantern. The only thing they could do was to firmly fix the time of the disaster. The last entry in the chief keeper's records had been made at 9am on Saturday, December 15th. As the morning's work seemed to have been completed, it was a safe assumption that the inexplicable 'occurrence' had taken place around lunchtime on the 15th. More than that they could not say. At dusk the *Hesperus* returned to Loch Roag still carrying its Christmas fare, having left Moore to keep his lonely vigil in the lantern room of the Eilean Mor light.

It was the longest two days Moore had ever spent. He lit the lantern and made himself a fire but the whole time he was haunted by the faces of the three missing keepers. Sometimes he was certain that he could hear their voices, but it was just the doleful cries of the sea-birds. Other times he was convinced that he could hear footsteps approaching the tower but, though he waited with bated breath, they never came inside. Always there was the relentless crash of waves against the rocks and the melancholy howl of the wind.

On December 28th a team of official investigators arrived at the Flannans to organize a new search, starting at the eastern jetty. Everything there was just as Moore had left it on December 26th, with ropes and lifebelts stored carefully away. At the western jetty there was some gale damage but, considering the weather conditions for the last ten days, no one was really surprised or concerned by this. Also at the western jetty, sixty feet above water level, was a crane on a concrete platform. In spite of the apparent ferocity of the gale it was completely undamaged – even its canvas cover was still lashed securely and knotted with rope. The curious thing about the crane was that odd bits and pieces of rope were draped over it for no reason that anyone could understand. Moore told them that there was a tool-box full of spares for the crane about 110 feet up the cliff face, and the ropes looked as if they could have fallen from there. One of the investigators climbed up to the rocky crevice and found it empty. The heavy box had completely disappeared! Was it possible that the island of Eilean Mor could have been battered by waves *110 feet higher* than sea level, waves strong enough to tear a heavy tool-chest from its moorings, casting some of its contents over the crane and the rest into the sea? It certainly didn't seem possible to Moore, with his experience of the islands, that waves could ever reach that height. Even if it were possible, he knew that only a madman would be anywhere near the jetty in such weather conditions. Experienced lighthouse-keepers stayed inside with doors and windows firmly secured at the first hint of bad weather. Their first priority, after all, was saving sailors' lives by keeping the lantern lit; it wasn't part of their job to wander about storm-swept cliff-tops, putting their own lives in peril. In any case, one keeper, Donald McArthur, wasn't even wearing his boots or his oilskins when he disappeared because they were still in a cupboard at the lighthouse.

After searching the rest of the island and finding no more clues, the investigators came to the conclusion that the three keepers must have been down on the jetty on the 15th, perhaps inspecting the crane, when a sudden freak wave had engulfed them and swept them off the platform. Apart from the fact that McArthur would never have been down there anyway without his boots and oilskins, it was the only possible explanation. Then someone remembered that December 15th had been a bright, calm day with no hint of gales or storms. Still it was perhaps possible that Ducat, the head keeper, had forgotten to fill in his log and that the 'accident' had taken place on the following day, the 16th, when it had been quite stormy. Moore, knowing his friends as he did, was not at all convinced but he couldn't think of a better solution, and so the investigators departed from the island to prepare their report. When they arrived back at Loch Roag, however, they found the steamship *Archer* waiting for them with very disturbing news. Apparently this particular ship had passed very close to the Flannans at midnight on December 15th and those on board were surprised to find that the light was not working. They were quite certain that not a glimmer of light had been showing on that particular day. This now meant that the three sensible, experienced seamen had been swept off the jetty in a howling gale on a calm, bright day. It made no sense at all!

All sorts of theories have been put forward in the following years. Perhaps one keeper went mad and murdered the others. Yet there was no sign of a struggle, nor anything missing that could possibly have been used as a weapon. He could, of course, have pushed them both into the sea at the same moment, but would he have thrown himself in as well? Also, bodies have a nasty habit of being washed up, sometime, somewhere. They weren't in this case. The local people, who knew more about the history of the Flannans than did the investigators, have a different theory which continues to be passed down from generation to generation. They say that an unseen force on the island of Eilean Mor would not tolerate intruders and got rid of them. They say that when Joseph Moore flung open the door of the lighthouse and called out the names of his friends, three enormous black birds the like of which have never been seen before launched themselves from the top of the tower and flew out to sea. As an explanation it certainly stretches the imagination. But is there a better one?

4 The flaming cross

It was the early hours of a very chilly October morning in 1967. Mr Christopher Garner, a farmer, was on his way home to Hatherleigh, near Exeter, Devon, when he found that he could hardly keep his eyes open. Realizing how dangerous this was, he pulled his Land-Rover off the road, wrapped himself in a blanket and settled down for a couple of hours' sleep. He was rather annoyed when his slumbers were rudely disturbed by a frantic knocking on his side window. He opened his eyes, only to close them quickly when he found the light of a torch glaring into them. When he eventually pulled himself together he found that the torch was being held by a grim-faced policeman. He threw the car door open, thinking that either he must be breaking some sort of parking regulation or that he had been mistaken for an escaped criminal. He was somewhat taken aback when the policeman, instead of interrogating him, smiled sheepishly and asked him to do him a favour.

Mr Garner asked him what the favour was. A second policeman pointed to the sky and asked the farmer if he could see anything unusual. The sky certainly seemed blacker than Mr Garner remembered it, but that was probably because he was comparing it with a group of lights which seemed to form themselves into the shape of a cross and then gradually moved off into the distance. The curious thing was that the lights seemed to expand and contract in rhythm as if they were throbbing inside!

The policemen, whose names were Clifford Waycott and Roger Willey, looked relieved when Mr Garner described what he could see, and they told him how shaken they had been when they first spotted the 'thing'. Apparently they had been driving along the A3072 between Okehampton and Holsworthy when they suddenly became aware of a pulsating formation of lights just above and to the left of them. When the policemen stopped and stared at it, the 'thing' also stopped and gave the creepy impression that *it* was staring back at *them*. When they started moving again it coasted along slightly ahead of them, gliding just above the tree tops and gleaming with a strange, incandescent glow. The policemen radioed their amazing news to headquarters and said they thought it would be a good idea for them to follow the glowing object until they discovered what it was. The driver of the police car then put his foot down hard on the accelerator in an attempt to close the gap between themselves and the odd object. Yet as he moved faster so did the 'thing', and soon the policemen found themselves careering about the countryside at as much as ninety miles an hour! When they realized that they were still no nearer to catching their quarry they turned around and went back to headquarters.

The newspapers gave the story wide coverage and the two bewildered constables and the third witness, Mr Garner, were inundated by reporters. A press conference was held later in the day and the officers were asked about their unusual experience. PC Waycott told the reporters that although the light wasn't piercing enough to hurt the eyes it shone with an unusual brilliance he had never previously encountered. A couple of minutes before it disappeared the officers had noticed another object, also large, silent and cross-shaped, gliding across the sky to join the first one before both had disappeared over the horizon. Both constables had been amazed by the speed of the object, which outpaced them easily when they were driving at speeds of ninety miles an hour. They thought that in some uncanny way it knew they were following it and was just as interested in their behaviour as they were interested in its odd behaviour!

It was suggested that this 'unidentified flying object' could have come from the nearby RAF station at Chivenor, but the people in authority there denied all knowledge of it. They had never heard of an aircraft that could fly as slowly as thirty miles an hour, accelerate to supersonic speeds, and yet also hover in one place if it felt like it. They had certainly never seen anything that looked remotely like the machine that the constables had described.

This heralded the beginning of a flying saucer 'scare' that lasted well over a week and threw people all over the country into a panic. Suddenly it seemed as if practically everyone had seen fiery orbs humming and glowing over Britain. A 'flaming cross' suspended over Glossop, Derbyshire, was seen by at least six sane and sober policemen, a Brighton bus driver saw a cylindrical green object flying over the sea at Saltdean, Sussex, and a Scottish coastguard claimed to have watched an object like a Catherine-wheel spinning over Wigtownshire. He said that it was humming and travelling at about 400 miles an hour.

A wing commander and his wife on a trip across Hampshire also saw the flashing lights. They said that although the lights formed a perfect V-formation when they first saw them, they later re-formed into the sort of cross that Waycott and Willey had followed. Wing Commander Cox had counted the lights and said that there were seven of them, all whitish yellow, bright, noiseless and exactly the same size. He also said, 'The night was clear with the moon just coming up and we were stone-cold sober!'

Another wave of excitement hit Britain and various people racked their brains to solve the identity of the strange craft. The Royal Observatory (in Herstmonceux, Sussex) thought that the planet Venus was the culprit, as apparently it shone extremely brightly in the eastern sky during the early mornings of October. Before this explanation had a chance to be accepted it was scotched by the report of Peter Barker, an amateur astronomer in Hastings. He said that he himself had seen a UFO well below cloud level and in a position that ruled out any possibility of its being Venus or any other planet. The observatory then issued the following odd statement: 'There is something up there which is not a star or a planet.' This, of course, confirmed everyone's wildest nightmares and, when the Ministry of Defence emphatically denied that the strange sightings could be accounted for by some sort of newly designed aircraft of theirs, rumours about invaders from space became rife.

An explanation came from an unlikely source, however. A vicar from Dorset, who had also seen the throbbing lights, said that they were obviously planes flying in close formation. A large light that he had seen in the middle must belong to a central tanker plane that was refuelling the others. The Ministry of Defence leapt on this explanation gleefully: yes, there were in fact several refuelling operations taking place in the West Country on the evenings in question. The American Air Force had also been refuelling over Scotland, and a US spokesman added that their operations had been carried out at 26,000 feet and with plenty of lights showing. Apparently their tanker had a row of bright lights strung under its belly and the other planes were also well lit as they circled around it.

Britain breathed a sigh of relief and tried to forget all the other things that had not been explained, like the cigar-shaped objects and the spinning Catherine-wheels. The relief was to be short-lived, however. Later in the week the Ministry of Defence withdrew its first statement and admitted that, after all, there hadn't really been any refuelling operations at the time of the sightings. Also, the US Air Force spokesman said that all their exercises took place between 5pm and 9pm, whereas the sightings of flaming crosses occurred between midnight and dawn! As if to illustrate the point, the formation of throbbing lights showed itself once again, this time to an ex-policeman in Lancing, Sussex. Mr Frederick Smith and his wife both saw it at 5.30am. 'It was a breathtaking spectacle,' they told reporters and said it reminded them of the Cross of Lorraine.

At the very same time a policeman in Bacup, Lancashire, saw a cigar-shaped craft lurking above his police station. Constable Earnshaw, the policeman in question, was puzzled when he found there was unusual interference on the station's short-wave radio. He went outside to examine the aerial and saw a space-ship hovering 250 feet above the police-station roof. He thought the strange craft was about fifty feet long and ten feet across. He was close enough to see portholes alongside and to hear a low whirring sound coming from it. The ship appeared to be metallic and gave off a bright glow. PC Earnshaw was not the only one to see it; two other policemen, Donahue and Reader, arrived on the scene and they all watched the UFO for at least ten minutes before it rose vertically and vanished. The sighting was obviously taken seriously by the Lancashire police who issued the following statement: 'We have had UFO reports before – but nothing like this. There has been no reasonable explanation but it was something definitely seen!'

This sparked off an avalanche of UFO sightings. More policemen and other shift workers claimed to have seen flying things in the early hours of the morning. Farmers, housewives, schoolboys, clergymen and many others saw an amazing variety of objects floating above Britain in the days that followed. Some were just pinpricks or fingers of light, others were described as fat saucers or flying rugby-balls, but there was no doubt in the minds of the people who saw them. They really were there! In fact in 1967 UFO sightings reached their highest peak for ten years. The Ministry of Defence looked into 362 reports of unidentified flying objects which came from all sorts of people and from every part of the country. Eventually Mr Merlyn Rees, then Minister of Defence for the RAF, was asked to give his explanation for the arrival of the UFOs. He appeared convinced that none of the unusual objects reported in the sky could be alien or even mysterious. He also said that Britain had a blanket radar coverage that extended to a great height and, apart from one or two unexplained lights, nothing unusual had been reported. Certainly nothing had led the Ministry of Defence to believe that we were under the threat of invasion from Martian aliens!

That seemed to be the end of it – as far as most people were concerned anyway. Yet I don't suppose PCs Waycott and Willey were too happy about it, or the 361 other people who knew that they had seen something which the Ministry of Defence said wasn't really there. After all, it does seem unlikely that two down-to-earth policemen, experienced in night-duty conditions, should suddenly start chasing at ninety miles an hour a small light in the sky or even the planet Venus. And what about their eye-witness, Mr Garner the farmer? Everyone knows that the planet Venus doesn't cruise along skimming the tops of trees, yet if it were a hovering supersonic spacecraft, why didn't it make any noise? We don't seem to know the answers to these questions now, but maybe one day the flaming cross will be seen again and this time it might come close enough to be positively identified.

5 The riddle of the Oak Island money pit

The story of the Oak Island money pit is certainly the most intriguing I have come across concerning buried treasure. Usually tales of hidden gold are fairly straightforward. The loot is buried in the ground, a map of the location is made, sometimes the treasure is dug up again, sometimes the map is lost and it isn't. At least one person is usually killed as a result of greed for the gold, for however much treasure there is, no one ever seems to want to share it with anyone else! This story is not like that at all, which is what makes it so unusual.

It started in October 1795 when three young woodsmen, Smith, Vaughan and McGinnis, took a trip in their canoe on Mahone Bay, Nova Scotia. The bay itself is twenty miles long by twelve miles wide and contains 365 tiny uninhabited islands. The young men were attracted by one particular island that appeared to be covered with wild oak trees instead of the spruce that normally grew on the other islands. It was most unusual to find live oaks in that part of the country. They decided to land on the island and take a look, and to their great astonishment they found embedded in the rock a heavy iron mooring ring large enough to secure a sailing ship. Walking to the centre of the island, they found a really magnificent oak standing alone in a clearing. When they drew closer they realized that it was covered with odd marks and figures, and one branch, sixteen feet from the ground, had been sawn off four feet from the tree trunk. The bark on this branch had been almost worn away by rope burns as if it had been used as the centre of a pulley. The most exciting thing, however, was a large circular depression in the ground under the sawn-off branch where someone had obviously been digging. To these young men this could only mean one thing – pirates and buried treasure!

They came back the next day with picks and shovels and began what was to be a much longer dig than they expected. First they discovered a circular man-made shaft thirteen feet across. After digging for ten feet they came to a platform made of oak logs whose ends were embedded in the side of the pit. Thinking that this must be the lid of the treasure-trove, they tore the logs away greedily, but underneath was only the same hard-packed clay. Stifling their disappointment, they carried on digging. At twenty feet they found another log platform and at thirty feet another one still. By then they were feeling really disappointed. The digging had taken several weeks and winter was now approaching. They realized that they would now have to wait until spring and even then they would need expensive machinery if they were to dig any deeper.

They returned to the mainland and tried to raise money

among their friends to buy equipment. No one was at all interested and some of the older inhabitants even swore that the island was haunted. In spite of this, Smith and McGinnis married local girls and made their homes on Oak Island, still dreaming of the fabulous riches beneath their feet.

In 1803 they recommenced digging, using buckets and pulleys. They penetrated to eighty feet, finding a layer of oak logs marking each ten feet. At ninety feet they found a layer of ship's putty, and below this a stone covered with strange markings. As no one could understand them, Smith took the stone and built it into the walls of his house. They doggedly carried on digging and, at ninety-eight feet, their spades again struck something very hard. It was already dark so the two friends decided to leave their discovery until daylight. It was perhaps fortunate that they did, for the following morning they found that the pit was filled with sixty-five feet of water!

Perhaps grief and disappointment clouded their judgement, because at this point Smith, Vaughan and McGinnis made a mistake. Instead of sitting down and trying to reason out where the water had come from (for it was odd, after all, that such a vast quantity of water should appear from nowhere), they decided to try to bale it out by hand!

Weeks of baling made no impression at all (something else they should have considered peculiar) and so, going to a great deal more effort and expense, they dug another pit next door to the money pit, hoping by doing so to drain the water out of the first pit. They dug to a depth of 110 feet and then tunnelled under the original pit. Then the bottom of the old pit collapsed and the water gushed out, almost drowning them. By morning the water was up to sixty-five feet in both pits! This disaster tolled the death knell for the syndicate and they went bankrupt. Smith and McGinnis continued to live on the island with their families, but by the time the next syndicate of treasure-seekers had been formed they were both dead.

This second syndicate was formed in 1849 and it was made up of three local businessmen who had become intrigued by the thought of the hidden wealth. Before starting on a project which could be very costly, they decided to try a new drilling method which would give them a good idea of what was in the still-flooded pit before they commenced digging. They drilled to a level of 108 feet, ten feet farther than the previous syndicate had dug, and the drill encountered another layer of oak. After this it travelled through some sort of loose metal for twenty-two inches. When they brought the drill up again, tiny links of gold chain were stuck to the end of it. The experiment was repeated several times and a clear picture was built up of the contents of the pit. There were apparently two oak chests, one on top of the other, each containing some sort of loose metal that seemed very much like gold coins. After their original bright idea, the second syndicate unfortunately made the same foolish mistake as the first and dug a third pit next to the other two. After digging for 110 feet they tunnelled under the original pit and once again it collapsed, leaving the third pit flooded.

At long last one of the pit workers noticed that the water in the pit rose and fell with the ebb and flow of the tide. As it was obvious that sea water could not penetrate the thick island clay, it suddenly became very clear what was happening. The water had been channelled into the pit by unknown human hands! When the original treasure-seekers had dug to a certain depth they had triggered off a marine booby-trap which had flooded sea water into the pit to prevent anyone digging any deeper. A party was organized to search the beaches, and in no time at all under a mat of vegetable fibre they discovered five large drains spread in the shape of a fan. The drains acted as a reservoir for the sea water, which drained down a long inland channel. This filled the money pit and kept it topped up every day. What cunning people were these who would go to such lengths to protect their treasure?

At least the syndicate now realized that they needed to cut off the sea if they were to drain the pit, so they built a dam across the beach to prevent the reservoir being filled up at high tide. But the tide came up higher than usual one night and the dam collapsed. So did the second syndicate – it too went bankrupt!

For thirty years the pit was left to keep its secret. Then in 1893 another local businessman, Frederick Blair, formed a third syndicate to attempt the recovery of the treasure. Blair's men began by carefully dynamiting the openings in the secret water channel. This worked very well and the sea no longer rose and fell in the pits. As the whole area was now one vast overgrown bog and no one knew where the money pit used to be, the third syndicate also needed to do some drilling and investigating before they started to dig. They eventually found the original shaft, and came to the same conclusions about its contents as the second syndicate. However, they were not so hasty as their predecessors and carried on drilling beneath the two wooden chests. Underneath the chests they found the hard-packed blue clay again, but they kept drilling until they reached 151 feet. There the drill bit into what seemed like soft stone. They had some of it analysed and found that it was man-made cement, so they carried on digging in great excitement. It appeared that they had come to a cement chamber filled with gold in the shape of bars and coins. The two wooden treasure chests of gold placed higher in the shaft were obviously red herrings. The bulk of the treasure had been buried even lower down on the assumption that most treasure-seekers would be very content to take the chests and look no further. Underneath the chamber they found something not quite so pleasant. Suddenly water began to shoot up the drill pipe with incredible force – another booby-trap for unsuspecting gold diggers! A second underwater channel had been connected to the shaft by the people who built it. This time the prospectors pumped dye down the drill pipe and found the dye reappearing at the mouth of another man-made drain on a beach at the other end of the island.

Blair's men carried on drilling through more blue clay but finally ground to a halt at 170 feet when the drill bit into a layer of iron. As far as we know, no one has ever discovered

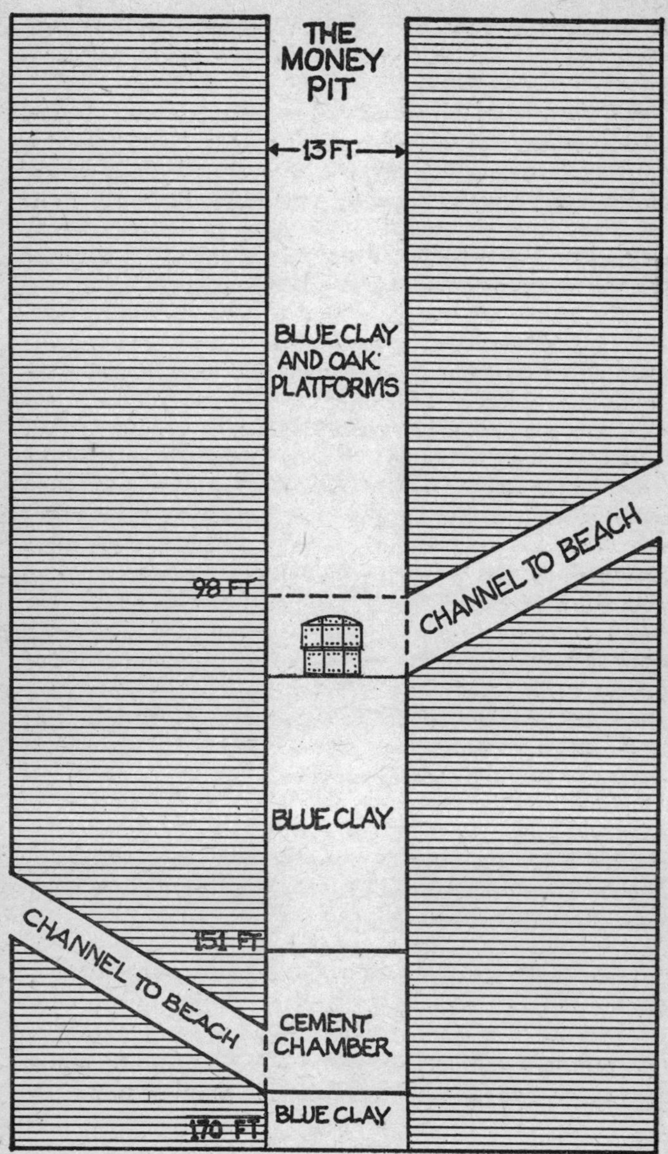

A plan of the money pit

what was beyond that. Blair's discoveries were really exciting, for they now knew without a doubt what they could expect to find in the pit, both the nice things and the nasty things. Yet in spite of that, they were not an inch nearer to getting their hands on the money than McGinnis and his men had been many years before. Blair and his men worked in the area on and off for fifty years, but the water-logged pits had long since collapsed into each other and the vast quantities of thick mud made digging a nightmare. And still the sea continued to filter through!

In 1935 an American, Gilbert Heddon, brought in very up-to-date and efficient machinery which was powered by electric cable from the mainland. He set to work to drain the pits by electric pumps which really did work for short periods, but it was impossible to keep the sea back for long. It was an expensive, unrewarding business and he soon gave up. Since then fortune-hunters have come to Oak Island every summer and have wasted a great deal of money and effort and gone home empty-handed. The gold is quite certainly still there, but indiscriminate digging has turned the underground workings into a sea of uncharted mud. Nowadays it would take a great deal of money just to find the treasure by boring, let alone digging for it.

But what of the people who put the treasure there? Who were they and how did they come by such a vast quantity of gold? And if they went to such trouble to hide it, why did they never return to dig it up again? The most curious thing is the fact that none of these mysterious unidentified people (and there must have been at least several to construct a pit of that size and complexity) ever breathed a word about it to anyone. There is also the strong iron ring which suggests that a large (pirate?) ship carrying many men had tied up on the island. Perhaps the men weren't allowed to live to tell the tale – yet the person who killed them, perhaps the leader, must have realized that he would need their help to reclaim the treasure. If we knew who he was, we might find the answer to the greatest treasure-trove mystery of all time.

6 The creeping coffins of Barbados

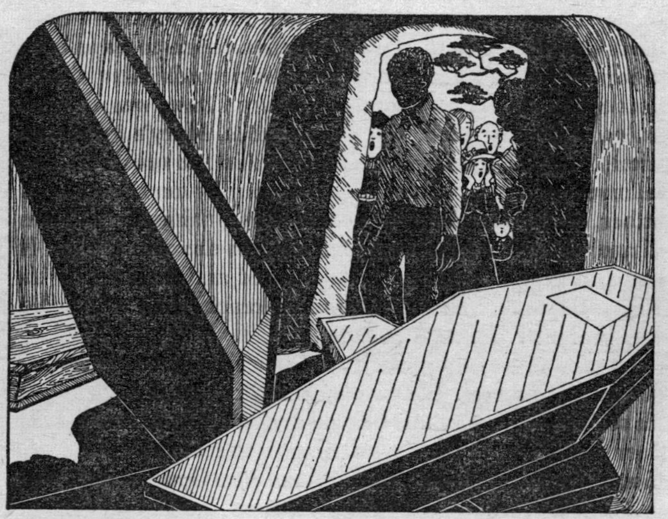

Standing in the little churchyard of Christchurch in St Oistin's Bay, Barbados, are several old stone vaults built over two hundred years ago. Weathered by warm winds and the hot Caribbean sun, there is little to distinguish one from another. Only one of these tombs has no door or other barrier at its entrance. Inside it is empty and deserted, abandoned for all time by the dead people it was supposed to guard, for this tomb was no place for the dead to rest in peace! It was originally hewn out of the solid limestone rock of St Oistin's Bay. The upper half was constructed from enormous blocks of coral-stone firmly cemented together. It is twelve feet long by six feet wide and tapers slightly towards an arched roof. The door, made from a massive slab of blue marble, was set into one of the sides. In fact the tomb just couldn't have been built more solidly had it been meant to house gold bullion instead of the remains of the departed!

The vault was built in 1724 for the body of the Honourable John Elliot. As far as the parish records show, his coffin never arrived and the vault lay empty for eighty-three years. The first burial, according to the church register, took place on 31 July 1807, when the coffin of a Mrs Thomasina Goddard was placed in it. The vault then seems to have been inherited by another family because records show that a new coffin, that of an infant girl, Mary Chase, was interred on 22 February 1808. On 6 July 1812 Mary's grown-up sister, Dorcas Chase, was also interred in the vault and was followed on August 9th of the same year by her slave-owner father, the Honourable Thomas Chase himself. Thomas Chase was not the most popular man in the community. It was said at the time that he was feared and detested by his Negro slaves and that his inhuman cruelty had driven his own daughter Dorcas to suicide.

In spite of his unpopularity many leading citizens turned out for the funeral. They stood in a silent semi-circle while his strong Negro servants heaved and strained at the marble door of the vault. Then a startling sight met the eyes of the mourners. For although the coffin of Mrs Goddard was still in its place, those containing Dorcas and Mary Chase seemed to have been lifted from their places and hurled against the opposite wall. The bereaved relatives were outraged, thinking it must be the work of grave robbers, but when a thorough investigation of the tomb revealed that nothing was missing they decided that someone must have played a very spiteful trick on them. The coffins were put back in their places and Thomas Chase's heavy coffin was lifted into the vault by eight bearers. The tomb was then carefully re-sealed and after a few days the whole affair had blown over. Four years later in September of 1816, when another funeral procession trudged its hot and weary way up the hill to the graveyard, the unpleasant incident at the previous burial had been almost forgotten.

This time it was the tiny coffin of Samuel Brewster Ames that was to be housed in the vault, and the mourners were in for another shock. When the vault was opened, again with great difficulty, the pall-bearers found that all the coffins, except that of Mrs Goddard, had been scattered about in crazy confusion. No one could imagine any reason for it! The coffins were again returned to their original places, the walls, roof and floor of the vault were examined thoroughly, and the mourners trudged home stunned and bewildered. Stonemasons were then called to cement the marble door back into position. For the next two months the evil spirits of the tomb were all the Barbadians could talk about, and when the body of Mr Samuel Brewster was carried up to the vault, on 17 November 1816, great crowds of curious sight-seers gathered to watch the opening. Samuel Brewster's burial would probably have attracted some morbid observers anyway, for he was a white man who had been brutally murdered in an unsuccessful uprising of Negro slaves. The fact that a murdered man was now being buried in this particular tomb made it an event no one wanted to miss!

The shocked members of his family stood in tense silence as the slab was once more pulled back and several pairs of curious eyes peered fearfully into the gloom. The five coffins, including the massive lead-lined one of Thomas Chase, were propped up against the walls, crossing and overlapping each other. Once again the only one undisturbed was the wooden coffin of Mrs Goddard. Several members of the funeral party made the usual detailed examination of the tomb and found no clue as to how anyone had entered. The whole place was as tight as a drum and as dry as snuff and by all appearances should have been as safe as a bank! Once more the coffins were replaced and the entrance slab cemented into position. From that day onwards the graveyard and its eerie tomb became one of the biggest sightseeing attractions on the island. Parties of horror-seeking trippers congregated daily in Christchurch cemetery gazing with unbelieving eyes at the impassive stone vault and gossiping with the local people on the fascinating subject of the cursed tomb. St Oistin's was rather an uneventful sort of place so the locals were always delighted to give their version of the creepy story. The white people usually blamed the black slaves and the black slaves usually blamed evil spirits. Yet no one seemed to have a theory with a grain of proof in it. During the days that followed, excitement mounted to fever pitch and finally the Governor himself, Lord Combermere, decided it was time to take a hand. He listened to reports of the affair, interviewed several witnesses and promised that he would be there in person to supervise the next opening of the vault.

Three years passed before the eagerly awaited day arrived. On 17 July 1819 a woman, Mrs Thomasina Clarke, presumably a relative of the Chase family, was to be buried in the vault. The funeral couldn't have been better advertised or attended had they been burying the King himself. Crowds lined the route taken by the funeral cortège and the graveyard itself was almost full of people. Lord Combermere and two of his staff took up positions near the marble door of the vault. In spite of the large numbers of people crowding the cemetery it would have been possible to hear a pin drop. The nervous stonemasons once more began their task of chipping away the cement seal. When the entrance slab was drawn back a familiar sight was revealed. Apart from Mrs Goddard's coffin which lay where it had been left, the other coffins had been scattered higgledy-piggledy and upside-down on the floor of the vault. A huge sigh rippled through the waiting crowd as the funeral party surged backwards in fright. Once more an unseen force had desecrated the Chase family vault. Lord Combermere was not so easily scared. A sober, practical man who had fought alongside Wellington in the Peninsular wars, he had no time for superstition. He pushed his way through the mourners and took a determined step into the burial chamber, while the others crowded behind him, lowering their lanterns. An unearthly coldness met them, making their spines tingle and their hair stand on end. They called for more lanterns and checked the vault more carefully than ever before. They came to the conclusion that there wasn't a chink big enough for a mouse to get in, let alone anyone big enough to fling lead-lined coffins around. Lord Combermere was utterly baffled!

It took several strong men to put the heavy coffins back into order again. After that, on Combermere's instructions, they sprinkled a layer of white sand all over the floor of the vault, hoping that on the next opening it might show footprints or some other marks that would give a clue to the mystery. This time the marble door was even more firmly cemented and Combermere made several impressions in the cement with his personal seal. Various other people came forward, including the rector of the parish, and made their own impressions in the cement. Whatever else happened, Combermere was now absolutely certain that no living creature could enter that room without leaving a mark. In the months that followed, excitement remained at fever-pitch and every possible solution to the mystery was thoroughly considered and then discarded. The rumours and speculation surrounding the vault became wilder week by week and many people, particularly the Chase relatives, found the whole affair a great strain.

After nine months, on 18 April 1820, Lord Combermere decided the matter must be settled once and for all. He gathered a group of important local dignitaries, the Honourable Nathan Lucas, Mr R. Bouchier Clarke, Mr Rowland Cotton and the Governor's secretary, Major J. Finch. Together they made their way to Christchurch to ask the rector, the Reverend Thomas Orderson, for permission to reopen the vault. The Reverend Orderson joined them and, along with a group of unhappy Negroes press-ganged from a nearby plantation, they set off for the churchyard. The events which followed were carefully written down by at least three of the party, Combermere, Orderson and Lucas, just to make absolutely sure that there could be no mistake.

To begin with, they spent a considerable amount of time examining the outside of the tomb. It was as solid as ever. Nathan Lucas tells us that 'the cement was uncracked and the large impressions of the Governor's seal were as sharp and perfect as on the day on which they were made. Each

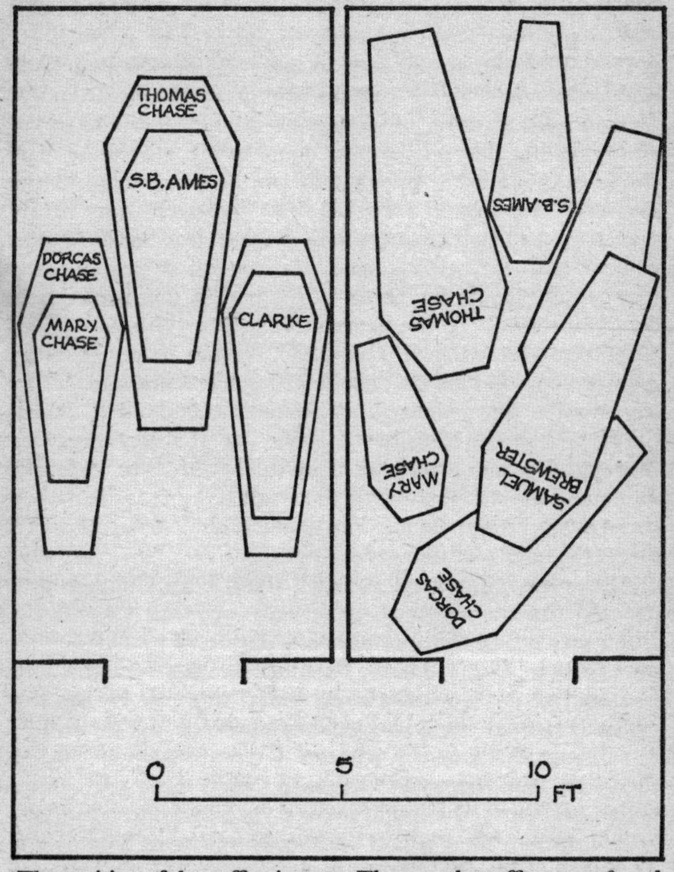

The position of the coffins just before the vault was sealed on 17 July 1819

The way the coffins were found after the vault was opened on 18 April 1820 person present, who, on the former occasion, had made his private mark, satisfied himself that it had not been tampered with.' The poor slaves, who would rather have been anywhere than the graveyard at this moment, reluctantly began to chip away at the cement again. This time, however, the marble slab seemed quite immovable, and it was discovered that something was jamming the door. The 'something' turned out to be one of the lead-lined coffins standing on its head! When the door was gradually eased open, it was immediately obvious that the coffins had been strewn about in the same confusion as before, with Mrs Goddard's once again the only one left untouched. The Governor stood on the bottom step with the rest of the party peering over his shoulders. The layer of white sand lay completely unmarked!

This is what Nathan Lucas wrote at the time: 'I examined the walls, the arch and every part of the vault, and found every part old and similar; and a mason in my presence struck every part with a hammer, and all was solid. I confess myself at a loss to account for the movement of these leaden coffins. Thieves certainly had no hand in it; and as for practical wit or hoax, too many requisite to be trusted with the secret for it to remain unknown, and as for the Negroes having anything to do with it, their superstitious fear of the dead and everything belonging to them precludes any idea of this kind. All I know is that it happened, that I was an eye-witness of the fact!'

Lord Combermere left the vault white-faced and shaken and within a few hours had signed an order for the vault to be emptied and the coffins buried in another part of the churchyard. He thought it was high time that the dead were allowed to rest in peace. The order was carried out at great speed and the tomb was never used again. Today the vault, a monument to its builders, stands as massive and as firmly cemented as ever. Beneath the dust and dead leaves the rock floor is still firm and unyielding, and even with today's aids to detection it is difficult to find any natural reason for the odd events that took place in a Barbados cemetery 150 years ago.

There are, however, two 'natural' explanations which perhaps are worth considering. The coffins could have been disturbed by repeated earthquakes. This theory was discarded at the time because it would mean that the earthquakes had been confined to the same 72-square-foot area each time, for earthquakes had not been felt anywhere else on the island. The other possible solution is that an inrush of flood water might have lifted the coffins and moved them them around the vault. Unfortunately no water marks were noticed at any time and the position of the vault on the top of the headland makes flooding very unlikely. Nathan Lucas's report tells us: 'There was no vestige of water to be discovered in the vault; no marks where it had been, and the vault is in a level churchyard, by no means in a fall, much less in a run of water!' In any case, surely water would have moved Mrs Goddard's wooden coffin around in much the same way as the others?

There is only one real clue to this strange mystery: only the coffins of the Chase family and its relatives were interfered with. Perhaps it was the alleged cruelty of Thomas Chase or his daughter's suicide that made someone, or 'something', hate them enough to play a repeated and very nasty practical joke. As we know so little about the family's history, it is difficult to come to any real conclusions about this. With so few possible solutions to consider, one theory seems to be as good as another!

7 The incredible affair of the dancing furniture

Henry Robinson was an eighty-six-year-old invalid. For twenty-five years he had lived as a tenant in a house at 8 Eland Road, Battersea, with his three daughters, his son and his grandson. His son, Frederick, and two eldest daughters, Lilian and Kate, were unmarried teachers, and his third, widowed daughter, a Mrs Perkins, looked after him and ran the house. She had a son of fourteen called Peter Perkins. Life had always been slow-moving and contented at No 8 and Mr Robinson considered himself a lucky man to be surrounded and cared for by his entire family. Then suddenly something happened which was to shatter their peace for all time. On 29 November 1927 copper coins, coal and pieces of soda began to rain on their conservatory roof!

At first the family were just startled, but as the deluge of odd objects showed no sign of stopping, one of them ran out to call a policeman. The panes began to crack under the strain of the fierce onslaught and splinters of glass began to fall on the frightened people below. A policeman eventually arrived and joined the group, who were now watching from outside in the garden. He also was astonished by the torrent of objects and became even more alarmed when a piece of coal, fiercely flung, actually knocked his helmet off. Galvanized into action, he hurled himself up on to the garden wall to get a good view of the surrounding houses, but he could see no one – and meanwhile the shower of missiles continued to bombard the conservatory roof.

It did stop eventually, but the policeman was so unnerved by what he had seen that he persuaded the local police force to keep a day-and-night vigil on the house. All was quiet and almost forgotten until December 19th, when the washerwoman who had been employed by the Robinsons for years gave in her notice. Shaking with fear, she took her employer to see a pile of cinders glowing in the outhouse. There was no fire nearby from which they could have come and yet they were far too hot to touch.

Less than a week later things really began to happen at the Robinsons'. For a whole hour loud bangs were heard in every room, window-panes cracked, lamps toppled and books and ornaments fell to the ground. The elder Mr Robinson who was, of course, unable to get out of bed unaided, began to shout out in terror as pieces of furniture literally began to dance up and down around him. His son Frederick ran upstairs to help, but by this time objects were hurling themselves against the wall and smashing into pieces. Frederick opened his father's bedroom door and as he did so the entire window, frame and all, burst into the room. It was as if the whole house were under bomb attack. Frederick just couldn't manage to evacuate his father alone, so he ran out into the street and grabbed hold of the first passer-by he saw, a Mr Bradbury. Together they heaved Mr Robinson out of bed and carried him downstairs. When Mr Bradbury saw a very large chest of drawers begin to dance and then fall over on its face, he very nearly dropped the invalid!

The terrified family most of whom were now gathered in the hall, along with Mr Bradbury, then saw the hall stand come to life. Frederick says that, hearing his sisters' screams, he grabbed it and tried to hold it down, but, he says, 'Some strange power seemed to tear it from my hands and it fell against the stairs. It broke into two parts!' Afterwards Mr Bradbury told police that Lilian Robinson desperately wanted to leave the house for ever but was too afraid to go up to her bedroom to pack her belongings. When things returned to normal again, a doctor was called for the old man who was then taken to hospital suffering from severe shock.

On January 14th there was a repeat performance. This time it brought down the conservatory and smashed the glass into tiny fragments. A freelance journalist, who happened to be passing on her way home, heard an explosion and shouts and rushed in to offer her help. When she saw the damage and heard the full story from the family, she lost no time in selling the amazing story to the national press. From then on, reporters descended on Eland Road in droves. There were also photographers, ghost hunters, people who were interested in the supernatural and people who were just plain nosy. If the Robinsons had troubles before, they certainly had a lot more now. In the days when they just had the 'thing' in the house they had some weeks at least when nothing happened and life was almost normal. Now there was no peace at all.

People knocked on their door day and night. Probably the most welcome visitor they had was a Mr Harry Price, a well-known expert in psychical research and an investigator into the unknown. He guaranteed to find an explanation of some sort, however disturbing, and was excellent at spotting anything faked. Price spent three hours talking to Frederick Robinson and he then made an inspection of the house with a reporter from the *Evening News*. While they were there Price and the reporter observed at least one object being hurled across a room by an unseen hand. Price seemed particularly impressed by what he had seen and was horrified to hear a day or so later that Frederick Robinson had been committed by the authorities to a mental hospital and was suspected of being responsible for all the damage himself.

Yet Frederick's enforced hospitalization did nothing to stop the invisible demon. The day after he left, a Saturday, Mrs Perkins told of chairs marching down the hall in single file, and on Sunday as she had tried to put the lunch out the same chairs had danced on the table and scattered all the dishes and cutlery. When she finally managed to prepare the lunch, the whole table had turned slowly over on to its side and deposited the food on the carpet. When Price called at the house on Monday morning, Mrs Perkins seemed to be near collapse and even young Peter, who at first had enjoyed the whole thing, looked tired and ill. The Perkinses were too terrified to sit down, let alone sleep. Price was now convinced that for some reason the Robinsons were being haunted by a poltergeist or 'mischievous ghost'.

Lilian had also had enough; she snatched up a few clothes and left the house in a thoroughly demented state. Peter was then sent away by his distracted mother. He was to stay with relatives in the country until things calmed down. The two remaining sisters were told by police to close up the house for a few days. They were glad to do this, thinking it would give their uninvited tormentor a chance to leave. They went to stay with friends several miles away and returned on January 25th accompanied by a well-known lady medium, a Mr Salisbury of the *Daily Express* and Mr Harry Price.

The medium was very unhappy about the house and

declared that she found it icily cold, although there was a fire roaring in the grate at the time. The investigator and the reporter spent the afternoon making a thorough examination of the house and furniture. While they were examining the last bedroom, they heard a thud outside the door and in the corridor outside they saw a large tablet of yellow soap that had not been there when they entered the room. The sisters, who were downstairs in the kitchen at the time, swore they had heard nothing and had not moved from the fireside. Later that day a dejected Frederick Robinson was allowed home from the mental hospital. He had been examined by several doctors who had declared him completely sane. He was very bitter about his unjust imprisonment and was now determined to get his sisters out of the house and away from the source of the trouble as soon as possible. The Robinsons immediately began to pack whatever they could find that was still in one piece and within a few days they had left the house – for good! Old Mr Robinson had also seen the last of No 8 Eland Road, for he never recovered from his shock and died in hospital.

Newspapermen still pursued the Robinsons, hoping for a statement that would help to clear up the whole mystery, but the Robinsons just wanted to forget the whole thing and get back to being a normal family again. For thirteen years they kept silent. Then on 14 March 1941 Frederick Robinson gave an account in *Two Worlds* of the weird happenings at his former home. He was obviously under the impression that the house had been haunted, and he talked about slips of paper that had fluttered down 'out of nowhere'. Some of them had spidery writing 'as if done with a pin' and were from two people who claimed to have been born during the reign of William the Conqueror. They signed themselves Tom and Jessie Blood! A romantic but unlikely story on the surface, though there is no doubt that something most peculiar did happen at the Robinsons' in 1928. There were too many reliable witnesses for it all to have been imagined. Could any of the effects have been achieved by trickery, and if so, what would be the point? The Robinsons, who had appeared perfectly normal until then, did not seem to welcome the publicity and certainly made no money out of it. Why would they put themselves to so much trouble and end up losing their father, their house and their peace of mind? The mystery has been investigated many times but remains unsolved.

8 The elusive monster of Loch Ness

Loch Ness, in the Highlands of Scotland, is the largest of a chain of three lochs which lie in a great furrow made thousands of years ago by a crack in the earth's crust. The lochs divide the Highlands from east to west. Loch Ness itself is a long, narrow lake, one or two miles wide and about twenty-four miles long, which forms part of the Caledonian Canal. In the Ice Age it was filled with glaciers which gave it its steep sides and very flat bottom, which is about 700 feet below the surface. The bottom is covered by a thick layer of mud and slime. Loch Ness has always been a lonely and desolate stretch of water. In the early days it was only ever seen by local fishermen from their boats and the very occasional traveller on foot or horseback who braved the path around the loch that was so difficult to negotiate. Even from the path itself it was impossible to see into the loch because of a thick screen of trees and bushes around the shore.

In spite of its peace and desolation, even then the loch had a reputation for housing a kelpie or water monster. Scots people have a great affinity with these large stretches of water and in Scots folklore many of these lakes had legends about Great Worms or Waterhorses. The Great Waterhorse of Loch Ness was said to be particularly large and black and first appeared as far back as the sixth century to St Columba, an early Christian missionary. While he was working up there he found it necessary to cross the River Ness, and when he arrived safely at the bank he found some of the local people burying a poor man who had apparently been attacked by a 'fearsome black beast' and savagely bitten to death. St Columba then told his companions to swim out and bring in the dead man's boat. One of them undressed and jumped into the water but the monster, which had been hiding on the bottom, swam up to the surface and chased the defenceless swimmer with its mouth wide open. St Columba made the sign of the Cross and shouted to the ferocious monster, telling it to go away. The monster, startled at being shouted at by a priest, quickly made off in the opposite direction.

Since then the existence in the loch of 'a very odd-looking beastie, something like a huge frog only it isn't a frog' was accepted by the local residents and the story has been passed down from generation to generation. Even as recently as 1810 children were warned never to play on the banks of the loch in case the monster came ashore and carried them away. A diver, Duncan McDonald, who was working on a submerged wreck in 1880, swore that a great creature had passed very close to him underneath the water! The water monster was reported occasionally in the years that followed, but the Highlanders were remote, secretive people and there may have been many glimpses of the monster that were neither talked about nor written down.

With the advent of motor cars, it was decided that a proper road should be built alongside the loch, linking Fort Augustus and Inverness. Work on it began in 1933. Heavy machinery, lorries and gangs of workmen then moved into the area and the peace of many centuries was soon shattered! It was not an easy task for the road builders as the highway had to be blasted out of the rocky mountainside. The noise of the dynamite was deafening and the sound of tons of displaced rock plunging into the depths of the loch could have awakened the dead. Who knows, perhaps it did – for some very curious things began to happen!

Men who were working around the loch at that time began to see a series of inexplicable 'things' swimming and wallowing just below the surface of the water. As these creatures moved they left behind a large V-shaped backwash like that of a speedboat. So many people reported seeing this phenomenon that the local papers began to take an interest and the first report was published in the *Inverness Courier* on 2 May 1933. On a sunny afternoon the previous week a Mr and Mrs McKay had been driving along the north shore of the loch towards Fort Augustus when Mrs McKay saw a large disturbance in the water. At first she thought it must be wild ducks squabbling, but as she watched the area of commotion became larger until two large black humps broke the surface one behind the other. The humps rose and fell in an undulating manner, but remained clearly on view. Mrs McKay watched for several minutes as the humps swam out to the pier and then, with more splashing and wallowing, they disappeared from view. Mr McKay, the driver of the car, stopped in time to see the large waves made by the humps come rolling into shore!

The report in the newspapers caused great interest, and the 'thing' in the lake very soon became labelled the 'Loch Ness monster'. Many people came forward and gave similar accounts of things they had seen in the loch. Another couple, a Mr and Mrs Spicer, claimed to have seen the monster actually out of the water and lumbering about in the road. As they drove towards it, it lurched back into the loch and swam away, leaving behind its V-shaped trademark! The Spicers said that it had a long neck which moved up and down in the manner of a scenic railway and the whole effect reminded them at the time of a prehistoric animal something like the Brontosaurus. Yet they said it moved with a series of jerks, like a giant snail. By 1934 excitement was really mounting. A veterinary student caught sight of the 'thing' from his motorbike. He said it was about twenty feet long with four webbed flippers. A passing chemist from Inverness was alarmed by the monster's large neck and strong threshing tail. Money prizes were offered for the capture of a real live Loch Ness monster, and Bertram Mills offered £20,000 for one he could use in his circus!

During the first two years of sightings it gradually became evident that many people in the rest of Britain also believed there was at least one huge, many-humped creature lurking in the loch. So in July 1934 a twenty-man team of observers was posted around the loch to gather the final batch of evidence which would prove the monster's existence once and for all. Apparently twenty-one photographs were taken of the creature in the loch, plus a ten-foot length of moving film. This evidence was shown to a team of scientists who decided that the unidentified animal was probably just a large grey seal. Somehow they couldn't manage to explain how a seal had got into the loch in the first place!

This discouraging opinion put an end to any further monster-hunting expeditions and people became reluctant to recount anything they had seen in case they were laughed at. The press, which had been the first to take the matter seriously, now treated the monster as a huge joke.

Then in 1939 World War II broke out and people turned their minds to other things. From the start of the war until victory in 1945 very little was heard of Loch Ness or its famous monster. Petrol had been far too scarce for people to go jaunting around the lochs in private cars, and in any case the Royal Navy was using Loch Ness for submarine testing and other research. It was at least ten years after the war ended before most people began taking long holidays again, but when the influx of tourists into Scotland rapidly increased, fresh reports were received of vast dark shapes swimming in Loch Ness and many more of the sinister V-shaped backwashes. Many people actually took photographs of the creature, but due to the dim light over the loch the pictures were not as revealing as they might have been.

One family, called Lowrie, were passing through the loch in a yacht when they saw and photographed an enormous beast coming to the surface only forty yards away from them. Overwhelmed by the size and closeness of the creature, they dared not stop to take more pictures but turned and made for the shore at full speed. A very clear V-shaped wake can be seen on the resulting photograph, but unfortunately there was no sign of the shiny brown-and-green neck and humps that the Lowries saw.

In 1960 Tim Dinsdale, a well-known and dedicated monster hunter who has written several books on the subject, took a moving film of the monster that was shown on television to about five million people. Apparently Mr Dinsdale had been in his car with a movie camera fixed on a tripod in place of the front passenger seat when he saw the sun glinting on something large and reddish-brown on top of the water. He stopped his car and looked through his binoculars and saw what he felt certain was the back of a great humped animal basking and wallowing in the water. He shot his film of the creature as it zig-zagged slowly across the loch, gradually submerging. Afterwards he could see quite clearly the large V-shaped backwash. Although his film was not very clear, it did serve to stir up a great deal more interest in the monster, and instead of being a joke it became respectable all over again.

In 1964 two special viewing platforms were built by the Loch Ness Investigation Bureau and one was placed on each side of the loch. A 35 mm movie camera was placed in the middle of the rig, flanked by two large still cameras. The idea was that the look-out would scan the loch through a telescope that had a cross-hair lens like that of a telescopic rifle. When he got the monster in his sights all the watcher had to do was press a trigger and the camera rolled into action! In spite of the efficiency of the camera, the project was not very successful. The monster was known to appear only on fine, warm days and during the time the platforms were manned, a period from Whitsun to October, there were only fifteen such days. Even so, vague, lumpy, wallowing shapes were seen many times, but on the whole the monster seemed to be giving the rigs a wide berth. When it was spotted it was always too far distant for a really clear film to be made.

Experiments were also tried using tiny submarines, but unfortunately the water always proved too murky and peat-stained for any photographs to be taken. However, some very interesting results have been obtained by using a scientific approach. On 20 July 1962 an echo-sounding expedition found a strange echo coming from a large unidentified object off Urquhart Castle. The results of the various experiments carried out by this team proved beyond a doubt that there *were* large moving objects in the loch and that they moved away rapidly when approached. The investigators also found numerous vast craters in the floor of the loch, and deep, steep-sided valleys many hundreds of feet long. In some places there was silt and mud up to eight feet deep. There is enough room here for several large beasts to hide, and more than enough fish in the loch for them to feed on.

It seems impossible to doubt that some strange water beast does inhabit Loch Ness and has done so for centuries. But what can it be? The most popular theory suggests that it is some species of extinct reptile, like a giant newt, that has managed to survive the passing of millions of years by hiding in this deep and desolate stretch of water. This theory is supported by a series of photographs taken by an American investigator, Dr Robert Rines, which were released in 1975. These pictures convinced a number of authorities, including

Sir Peter Scott and various museums in America, that a large aquatic beast did exist in the loch. Sir Peter Scott even went so far as to suggest a name for this species of monster – *Nessiteras rhombopteryx* – but some unkind person quickly pointed out that this is an anagram for 'monster hoax by Sir Peter S.'! Another theory says that the creature lives in the sea and swims into the loch by an underground route either to escape its enemies or just for the breeding season!

Do we really have a survivor from the prehistoric past here in Britain, or could it be just a Scots legend gradually exaggerated to boost the tourist industry? Most of us would love to think that the first explanation was true, but until we get more concrete evidence we can never be absolutely sure!

9 Flight into the unknown

In 1920 Amelia Earhart, an American, went with her father to an air show and watched in rapt amazement while the pilots performed their stunts in flimsy bi-planes. Before she left the display she was given a 'joyride' in one of the planes, and from that moment on she resolved to make flying her career. Although her father thought it was a huge joke, she enrolled for a course of flying lessons and three years later she was awarded her coveted international pilot's licence.

It was a mere piece of paper, but it gave her the freedom of the sky and she was now qualified to fly wherever she wished. She spent another three years doing just that and hoping to become established and respected enough to make a living from flying. However, women were not taken as seriously in those days as they are today. Although people were amused by the idea of a woman piloting a plane, it would have been unthinkable for anyone to give her a flying job if there were a man available. The fact that he might be less experienced or not as well-qualified made no difference at all. In 1926 she finally realized that she was not going to be accepted in this all-male stronghold so she gave up flying to become a social worker in Boston.

Then, quite out of the blue, she was invited to join the crew of the *Friendship*, an aircraft owned by another woman named Mrs Guest, which was to make a bid to cross the Atlantic. *Friendship* was a three-engined Fokker with floats underneath, and apart from the pilot and mechanic Amelia was the only person on board. It was a stormy, hair-raising trip, but in spite of ice on the wings and a coughing engine they arrived safely and had the distinction of being only the eleventh plane ever to cross the Atlantic! It was certainly a breakthrough for Amelia, for from then on every time she took to the air reporters and photographers were standing by to record the event. She rewarded their interest by breaking every flying record that she tried for.

After logging a thousand hours in the air, she decided the time had come to take the ultimate test: a solo flight across the Atlantic! It was the early summer of 1932 and she was now the proud owner of a single-engined Lockheed Vega painted a brilliant red. The daring American girl flew alone over a stretch of unbroken sea for fifteen hours until she caught the first glimpse of the Irish coast. She was the first woman to cross the Atlantic alone and had also done it in less time than anyone else. This feat started Amelia Earhart, the first lady of the air, on the way to becoming a legend! She had proved beyond a doubt that, given the opportunity, a woman could achieve the same flying skills and show the same qualities of bravery and endurance as any man. She was hailed as a heroine by women all over the world.

In 1935 she crossed the Pacific, and on 1 June 1937 she set out to encircle the globe. This was a trip she could not attempt alone, as she needed an expert navigator, and the man chosen to go with her was supposed to be the best. His name was Frederick Noonan and the plane they were to fly was a twin-engined Lockheed Electra monoplane called *Lady Lindy*. By the beginning of July they had flown a distance of 22,000 miles, with only 6,000 miles remaining to complete the circle. They stopped off at Lae in New Guinea to refuel, and by now both navigator and pilot were feeling very exhausted, yet still determined to finish their trip. Their next stop was to be Howland Island, a tiny dot in mid-Pacific and the last stepping stone to Hawaii and the United States. It was to take them twenty more hours.

Anchored off New Guinea to help *Lady Lindy* find the island was the US Coast Guard cutter *Itasca* which was in constant radio contact with the little plane. Unfortunately, for some reason there was a great deal of radio interference that day and most of Amelia's words just couldn't be heard. Finally they heard her anxious voice say 'Gas running low', and then the one word 'Circling'. To the crew on board the *Itasca* it meant only one thing. *Lady Lindy*, with probably the most experienced flying and navigation team in the world on board, had somehow completely lost her way. How could it have happened?

It was 8.45am on 3 July 1937 when her last transmission was picked up and after that there was complete radio silence. The little monoplane was expected to arrive on Howland Island by 8am; if she really were lost, she had at least four hours' flying time left, depending on the direction and strength of the wind. Amelia could still find Howland or a similar island in that time or, even if she came down in the sea, her empty fuel tanks should keep her afloat for hours or possibly days. Yet her mysterious radio silence continued, although the navy men knew that if she were still airborne her radio transmitter was capable of sending messages a distance of up to 1,000 miles. The captain of the US *Itasca* radioed Washington: 'Amelia Earhart missing.'

President Roosevelt gave immediate orders for a search, and this resulted in an aircraft carrier, six other fast ships and several planes combing almost a quarter of a million square miles of the Pacific Ocean. The sea was calm and the weather was fine but no trace of the Lockheed Electra was found, not even the smallest piece of debris. The news of their heroine's disappearance rocked the USA. No one wanted to believe that she was really gone for good and every possible alternative to her actual death was considered. Some said that Amelia (who was married to someone else) and Fred had fallen in love and instead of carrying on with their trip had flown to some remote, uninhabited island where they could be together. Rather a dramatic way of eloping!

A girlfriend of Amelia, who was also a pilot and an expert in extra-sensory perception, announced that the *Lady Lindy* really had crashed into the Pacific but fortunately very near a Japanese fishing vessel. She said that Amelia and Fred had been picked up and were at that moment being taken to Tokyo. This was 1937, only two years before the outbreak of World War II when America and Japan were to be bitter enemies. There was already much anti-Japanese feeling in the US and, as time passed and the two fliers didn't turn up, a new rumour began to spread. Amelia and Fred were not just pilots, they were US government spies! They had flown over Japanese territory in order to take photographs and had been shot down by Japanese anti-aircraft fire. No comment was made by the government and two years later an official verdict 'lost at sea' was recorded in court. Many people still believed that, as World War II progressed and the US Navy advanced through the Pacific islands, Amelia and Fred would be found in a Japanese prison.

In fact no trace of the aviators or their plane was ever found when the Pacific islands were eventually searched, and if the Japanese had had anything to do with the fliers' disappearance they had concealed their crime very carefully. Yet in 1944 in the Mariana Islands, just north of Howland, two Marines found a snapshot album containing clear photographs of Amelia Earhart in the same flying kit she had worn on the day she disappeared. Further investigation uncovered a very detailed file on Amelia at Japanese headquarters in Tokyo, as if the military authorities had had a particular reason for being very interested in her.

Gradually from odd rumours and bits of information a picture was built up of the possible end of Amelia and Fred. The crew of the *Lady Lindy* were probably shot down and captured by the Japanese and taken to the Pacific military headquarters at Saipan. Soon after her arrival Amelia had an acute attack of dysentery which caused her death, and Fred was subsequently shot for spying. Most of this story is based on rumour, yet some American Marines who were fighting in Saipan have a curious story to tell. Apparently during the Occupation they were given orders to dig up a mysterious unmarked grave in a native cemetery. The two unidentified bodies that were found there were then flown in unmarked coffins to the United States. Where were the bodies taken? Could they really have been the remains of Amelia Earhart and Frederick Noonan? If so, why was it kept a secret?

The last clue came to light in 1960 in Paul Briand's biography of the woman pilot. Apparently in 1946 a Japanese girl who was working for a naval dentist suddenly claimed that she had been in Tanapag when a silver two-engined plane crash-landed in the harbour on its belly. She said that she saw two people pulled out of it, one a man and the other a woman with short, curly hair who looked ill and tired. Although the dental assistant, whose name was Josephine Blanco, was only eleven years old at the time, she clearly remembered the Americans being taken into the nearby woods and shot. Yet this story seems to contradict the one that tells of the pilots being imprisoned in Saipan. Could the Japanese girl have been making the story up or just embroidering a rumour she had heard? If not, it seems strange that she said nothing about such a dramatic occurrence until nine years later!

The mystery of what happened to Amelia Earhart and her navigator in 1937 has never been satisfactorily explained, although it is obvious that the American and Japanese governments know more than they are saying. Will more evidence ever come to light? Or will Amelia's last trip always remain a 'flight into the unknown'?

10 The riddle of the *Mary Celeste*

In November 1872 the three-masted barque *Dei Gratia* sailed from New York bound for Gibraltar. She was hoping for good weather and an uneventful journey and would have been surprised to know that she was sailing into the middle of the most baffling sea riddle for a hundred years! On December 8th, a calm, sunny day, the *Dei Gratia* sighted a two-masted brigantine sailing on a starboard tack but in a strange and erratic fashion. The *Dei Gratia* caught up with the brig and signalled to her. The silent stranger yawed alongside and made no reply. The curious crew of the barque hung over the rails as she came in as close as she dared to the unidentified ship. The captain, David Morehouse, picked up the loudhailer and his voice boomed out across the narrow strip of water dividing the ships.

The stillness after the echo was uncanny. The sails still flapped and the timbers creaked and groaned as the waves slapped them, but there was no sign at all of human life. Were there any crew members on board? Were they all drunk below decks? Or dead? There was only one sure way to find out. The skipper had a boat lowered and he and the second mate and two of the crew rowed across to the ghost ship. As they rounded the prow they saw her name written on it: '*Mary Celeste* – New York'. The captain and his second mate reluctantly scrambled on board her, leaving the other two men in the boat. They stamped on the decks and shouted themselves hoarse but no one came up to greet them. The only moving thing on deck was the ship's wheel, which swung about aimlessly as if following its own whim.

The men searched the ship from stem to stern but found not a soul on board, not even a dog or a rat. Nor was there any clue to the crew's disappearance, for the *Mary Celeste* was sound, seaworthy and stacked with water and provisions. The private possessions of the crew were littered around their cabins as if their owners had just stepped out for a minute. Shiny razors lay ready for use without a hint of rust on them, and a line full of newly washed underwear hung dry and ready to put on!

In the ship's galley there were pans still containing traces of cooked food, and inside the stove they found the ashes of a burned-out fire. To the captain and his mate it looked as if the crew had been interrupted in the middle of breakfast, for the table was fully laid and the plates still bore the remains of porridge and half-eaten boiled eggs. A bottle of cough medicine stood on the table with a spoon beside it, its cork already removed, ready for someone to come back and take a dose! They also found a sewing machine with a child's dress still caught in it. Standing upright beside it was a thimble, a reel of cotton and a tiny bottle of sewing-machine oil. In the captain's cabin, besides the captain's clothing, they found dresses belonging to a woman, apparently his wife, and clothes for a small girl. There were toys too.

The two seamen found the whole situation increasingly creepy. The only possible explanation that they could think of was that the captain, his wife, child and the whole crew had rushed out on deck and jumped overboard at the same moment for no apparent reason.

As they continued their search they found a few things that disturbed them even more. All the cabin windows were battened with planks of wood and pieces of canvas – rather like a fortress. In the captain's cabin they also came across a sheathed cutlass which appeared to have been stained with blood and then hastily wiped dry. On the starboard top-gallant rail they found more apparent blood stains and a wedge-shaped cut that looked as if it had been made by an axe. Strangest of all and even more difficult to explain were the long, deep slashes which they noticed on each side of the ship's bows. The ridges were about an inch and a quarter wide and seven feet long and had obviously been carved deliberately and very recently. The officers of the *Dei Gratia* were now totally mystified. They read through the log of the *Mary Celeste*, hoping for a message of some kind, but found that no entries had been made since ten days earlier when the brig was recorded 420 miles from her present position. Could she really have sailed as far as that with a loose wheel and no hand to guide her? Nothing about it made any sense at all. Captain Morehouse and his mate were relieved to return to their own ship.

The mate, Oliver Deveau, later returned with two of the crew and prepared to navigate the derelict ship into port at Gibraltar. They reached there on 13 December 1872, a day later than the *Dei Gratia*. The brig was found to be an American ship owned by a Mr John Winchester, who was called across the Atlantic to claim her. He made a detailed examination of the cargo, which was alcohol, and pronounced it intact and quite untouched. He could throw no light on the mystery either, unless the crew had thought that the cargo was explosives and had jumped overboard because they were afraid of being blown up! Nobody took this story very seriously and Captain Morehouse was eventually awarded £1700 for salvage.

The arrival of the *Mary Celeste* at Gibraltar had caused a great deal of excitement and widespread speculation as to the fate of her captain and crew. The mysterious circumstances surrounding her abandonment were so unlikely that a hundred and one even more unlikely theories were produced to account for it. The most popular was that the crew had got drunk, murdered the officers and then were somehow captured and put aboard another ship. Any day now this rescue ship would sail over the horizon carrying the evil crew members clad in irons. Yet months went by and no one reported having seen or heard a word from the crew of the derelict brigantine. By this time the story had been turned the other way about. Captain Briggs of the *Mary Celeste* was probably a very religious man (he did after all have a harmonium and a bible in his cabin). Instead of the crew murdering him, he had massacred them, probably in a fit of religious mania. Afterwards he had thrown them all overboard, including his wife and baby, and just to keep things neat and tidy had jumped in himself. If this story is difficult to believe, there were many more tales just as unlikely.

Some swore that the seamen had been the victims of one of the sea serpents that were said to be around at that time. The monster in question could have just lurched out of the sea in front of the brig and then snapped up the captain and crew members from the decks. Or, alternatively, it could have been pirates or alien creatures from Mars! Yet it does seem rather odd that these dramatic happenings should leave no evidence.

Then bogus survivors began to turn up, usually eccentric cranks who thought that by telling the 'true story' of the *Mary Celeste* they would be able to step into the limelight. The most curious of these was an Englishman called Abel

Fosdyk who claimed to be the one and only survivor of the deserted brig. He said an accident had happened while the crew had been watching a race between the captain, Ben Briggs, and his mate. Apparently the captain had insisted on a rickety grandstand being erected around the bows in order that his little daughter should see more clearly. It was known as the 'baby's quarterdeck' and its building was supposed to account for the slashes on the sides of the bows. Apparently, while the race was in progress, a man-eating shark appeared, throwing everyone into a panic. In the general confusion the platform collapsed into the water, taking everyone with it. For some reason Abel Fosdyk found himself floating on a raft and remembered nothing until he found himself washed up on the Ivory Coast of West Africa! It certainly made an interesting yarn, but whether anyone believed it is quite a different matter.

Of all the various theories about the mystery only one can be seriously considered today, and that is, surprisingly enough, bad food! In the days of the sailing ships, provisions for seamen were notoriously inedible. Bad maggoty meat, biscuits with weevil beetles, and stale and sour flour. Stale flour has been known to attract a kind of poisonous fungus called ergot. Ergot is often fatal and usually affects people with a strange madness involving hallucinations and suicide attempts. It is just possible that if every person on the boat ate a piece of bread infected with ergot, they could all have gone mad and jumped over the side together. It does seem unlikely, but can you think of a better explanation of why thirteen people should disappear into thin air?

11 Borley Rectory: the most haunted house in England

In the stately homes of England ghosts are a cherished tradition. These elusive spirits are to be found not only in old houses but crumbling castles, musty churchyards and in ruined battlements as well. Whether these ghosts are real or whether they exist only in the minds of the people who see them is an argument that has raged on for centuries. However, it is probably true to say that the people who laugh loudest at haunted houses have never spent the whole of a dark, moonless night in one. They certainly wouldn't even smile after a night spent in Borley Rectory, a gloomy edifice said to have a ghost for each of its thirty-five rooms. Nothing remains of the rectory today. It was gutted by fire in 1939 and its shell was completely demolished in 1944.

Borley Rectory was erected in 1863 by the Reverend Henry Bull, who had been appointed local minister the year before. It was located about sixty miles north-east of London at the village of Borley, near Sudbury in Suffolk. It was a rambling and uncomfortable house and it always had a coldness that no number of roaring fires could dispel. In spite of its size Henry Bull had to add another wing in 1875 as the number of his children had now increased to seventeen and he obviously needed more space! The new wing converted the rectory into a rectangular building with a bricked courtyard in the middle. The Rev Henry Bull served his parish and lived in the rectory for thirty years and during that time nearly every sort of ghostly phenomenon was experienced there. Many actual figures were seen, the most persistent of which was a gloomy nun, in addition to a headless man, a figure in grey and a girl in white. Another popular ghostly visitor was a coach and pair which was said to have swept up and down the narrow lane leading to the house on many occasions!

The melancholy nun apparently caused the reverend gentleman so much annoyance that he actually had the window to the left of the front door bricked up. She distracted him from his reading by constantly peering through the glass at him! There were beautifully kept grounds outside the house which were shaded by large trees. There were also beds of flowers, a lawn and several little paths. It was on one of these paths that the nun was most frequently seen, not just by Reverend Bull but by a number of other people, not all of whom were members of the family. On one particular occasion on a hot July afternoon in 1900, three of the reverend's daughters, Mabel, Ethel and Freda, met the young nun walking along the same little path in the rectory grounds. One of the girls went to fetch a fourth sister, Elsie, who laughed to think that a ghost should walk outdoors on a hot summer afternoon! Yet when she came out into the garden she also saw the young nun, walking along with hands clasped in front of her and seemingly completely unaware of the four young women staring at her. Elsie, bolder than the rest, attempted to get closer, but the nun suddenly turned and stared at Elsie with a look of such intense grief that the girl stopped in her tracks. Then the nun vanished. Elsie saw her again on the same path about four months later, still looking extremely unhappy. The little path became known as 'Nun's Walk'.

Edward Cooper, the gardener at Borley Rectory, also saw the nun there often and so did a local carpenter called Fred Cartwright who passed the rectory gate daily on his way to work. This was as late as 1927, the year that the Reverend Harry Bull (Henry's son) died, and when Borley Rectory was uninhabited. Apparently Cartwright, who was a complete stranger to the community, observed the nun on several occasions without the least suspicion that she was a ghost. She usually looked most forlorn and he thought it odd that she should always be hanging about the rectory looking so sad and lost. It never occurred to him that she was anything other than a real person. He was certainly unaware of any cold or uneasy feelings when he saw her! It was only when he asked about her at the local inn that he discovered, much to his amazement, that the rectory was haunted by a melancholy nun. On Henry Bull's death in 1892 his son Harry succeeded him, and he also saw the nun on many occasions, along with his four sisters, his cousin, the gardener, the carpenter, the cook and at least a dozen other people. The coach and pair, one of the most unusual manifestations at Borley, was also observed by the gardener, Edward Cooper. He claimed to have seen it many times shining brilliantly in the moonlight. It always raced across the church meadows, through walls, trees and hedges and disappeared into a farmyard below. Harry Bull also saw it many times when he was head of the Bull household after his father's death.

Apart from the apparitions, a wide variety of unusual noises were often heard in the house and its grounds. As well as the galloping hoofs of the coach and pair in the lane, whisperings and a woman's voice could be heard in some of the rooms. There were also footsteps, bangs, bumps, creaks and knocking noises, doorbells ringing, doors opening and closing, dogs padding about and scratching at doors, people jumping and stamping, and the sound of smashing windows, falling crockery, rushing water and church music! Some of the rooms were sealed off and guards posted outside to prevent people from entering, but somehow writing still appeared on the walls, usually in the form of urgent pleas for help. Yet no one knew who it was that needed help or what to do about it.

After almost a lifetime spent at the rectory, the Reverend Harry Bull seemed to be very much at home with the ghosts and often told of the personal involvement he felt he had with them. He also said that if he were unhappy after his own death he would lose no time in coming back to haunt Borley Rectory himself! In fact after his death his ghost was seen many times by the wife of the rector who succeeded him. Harry Bull's death left a vacancy at the rectory that was difficult to fill. The post of parish priest was offered to at least a dozen men, but all refused. Finally the Reverend G. E. Smith and his wife agreed to take on the rectory and its phantom visitors in spite of warnings from the previous occupants. They were determined not to believe in the happenings at Borley and to make a completely fresh start there.

The first hint of things not being what they should was when the couple heard slow, dragging footsteps moving across the floor of an unoccupied room. Mr Smith decided to take action before things got out of hand and spent the following night sitting up in the haunted room armed with a hockey stick! Once again he heard it – the sound of feet in some kind of loose slippers slapping against the bare boards. The Reverend lashed out with his stick at the place where the sounds seemed to be coming from, but the stick just whistled through thin air. After a pause the phantom feet began to drag all over again. Two days later a servant girl gave notice because she saw a nun walking in the woods behind the house and also leaning over the rectory's front gate in the same way that she had been doing for years. Another servant saw the old-fashioned coach on the lawn, and apparently it was close enough to be distinguished for the brown shading of its horses.

An account of these happenings was published in the *Daily Mirror* and brought the well-known ghost hunter Harry Price to the scene. He was renowned for his ability to search out the real spooks and uncover the fakes. He was delighted to have such a formidable challenge with Borley Rectory's many different ghosts, noises and occasional flashing lights. He found the Borley Rectory of 1929 a very depressing place indeed, without the benefits of electricity, gas or even a mains water supply. He received no help at all from the Reverend Smith who, in spite of the disturbing noises that he had heard, still refused to believe that ghosts were responsible. Besides looking after his parishioners he was also kept busy looking after his front garden, for the rectory now seemed to be inundated with coachloads of ghost-hunting sightseers who were often determined to get into the rectory at all costs.

Price managed to talk to some of the Bulls who still lived in the district, and on one summer evening he and a newspaperman decided to establish an all-night vigil in the garden. Both said that they definitely saw a gliding shape on the Nun's Walk but could not say definitely what it was, as it vanished when they came close to it.

This was the beginning of a ten-year study by Price on Borley Rectory. In 1935, when the Reverend Smith could not bear the rectory any longer, Price decided to rent the house for a year so that he could move in himself and be on hand to observe the ghostly capers. He invited along lots of friends, researchers and other impartial observers and the bizarre activities seemed to increase with the size of the audience. Now stone-throwing, an activity typical of poltergeists, began to occur, and when Price and his friends had seances the table was said to have spelt out all sorts of amazing information.

A medium called Helen Glanville claimed to have been told during a seance that the house was haunted by the spectre of Marie Lairre, a nun who had been induced to leave her convent at Le Havre, France, to become the wife of one of the Waldergraves who lived in Borley Manor. In 1667, when she was nineteen, her husband strangled her and buried her body under the cellar of his home. Apparently the rectory had been built on the site of this demolished manor house. Price and the rector are said to have excavated in the exact spot that the medium had described, and there they found the jawbone of a young woman.

Price moved out and in 1938 the rectory was bought by a Captain W. H. Gregson. He began to regret the move when he lost two dogs in succession! On two separate occasions he went to investigate footsteps in the courtyard, taking a spaniel with him. Captain Gregson said, 'The dog stopped dead, and positively went mad. He shrieked and tore away, still shrieking.' Neither dog was ever seen again.

It was while Captain Gregson owned the rectory that it caught fire. A paraffin lamp fell over, apparently of its own accord, and as the house burned a policeman who rushed up to help saw at least two shadowy figures watching the inferno. The shell of the building continued to be haunted, and even when the ruin was razed to the ground one poltergeist seemed to be taking a long time to leave. On 5 April 1944, the day of demolition, Price was there with a journalist and photographer from the American magazine *Life*. They took a famous photograph which shows a brick from the house apparently hovering in mid-air.

After Price's death many people claimed that he had exaggerated and distorted the evidence of ghostly happenings at Borley Rectory in order to gain publicity for his book and radio broadcasts on the subject. It was also said that the earlier hauntings had been imagined by the Bull family, who really did believe in ghosts, and that Price had just enlarged on this for his own ends. Whether or not this is true, it still does not explain things like the dragging footsteps heard by Reverend Smith, who certainly didn't believe in ghosts, Captain Gregson's disappearing dogs, and the sad nun seen by the visiting carpenter who had never even heard of Borley Rectory. Perhaps Price did dabble in the happenings at that infamous house and distort evidence for his own ends, but there still seems to be a great deal that cannot be explained away so easily!

It seemed as if this would be the end of the Borley manifestations, but in June 1970 two sober citizens, Mr Potter and Mr Croom-Hollingsworth, saw the Borley nun again wandering over the site of the old 'Nun's Walk'. They watched her drifting through fences and bushes for eleven minutes. Mr Potter even threw a brick through her! Excited by this apparition, Croom-Hollingsworth decided to take a look at nearby Borley church, and the results of this investigation were seen and heard on a recent BBC television programme. Tape recorders which had been locked into the empty church recorded doors being opened and closed, heavy objects being hurled about and some very bloodcurdling sighs!

12 Orffyreus and his wheel of eternity

Despite all the scientific progress which man has made, all machines still conform to a basic scientific law. To get power out of machines, whether they are complex like the engine of a jet aircraft or very simple like a hand-operated water pump, it is necessary to put even more power or energy into them. Nowadays this energy is usually supplied in the form of a fuel such as gas, petrol or electricity, but it could equally well be horsepower or manpower. For centuries it has been the inventor's dream to build a machine that can create its own energy and does not need any outside force. To discover this would be to discover the secret of perpetual motion.

Throughout the ages inventors from all over the world have claimed to have found a machine that achieves the impossible. Eventually all have been exposed as swindlers or cranks with the exception of one, a temperamental, restless young man who called himself Orffyreus. Orffyreus was born Johann Ernest Elias Bessler in Saxony in 1680. The name Orffyreus was probably adopted by the young German in an attempt to draw attention to himself in the same way as pop stars do today. We know very little about his early life except that he studied theology, medicine and painting before turning his attention to the building of machines. It was also said that he was driven out of several countries because people thought he was a wizard!

His reputation was probably enhanced by his wild appearance, for he was said to be a giant of a man with long, shaggy black hair. It was around 1712 that he began to be known for his 'self-moving wheels' which he showed off at exhibitions. He displayed the first of these at Gera, in the province of Reuss. It was a wheel about three feet in diameter and four inches thick. After being started, this wheel apparently increased its speed until it could lift up a weight of several pounds. In spite of this impressive feat, Orffyreus seemed to have had very few admirers of his work; in fact there were many who called him a charlatan and a barefaced rogue. He seemed little daunted by this, however, and wandered off to Draschwitz, near Leipzig, where he made another, larger machine. From there he went on to Merseburg where he made a machine twice the size of his original one which could lift seventy boxes of stones. As in all the models he built, he was careful to keep the moving parts covered by canvas, for he was determined that no one should steal his amazing secret.

Finally, at the age of thirty-six, he became tired of roaming Europe and having his inventions laughed at, so he attempted to settle in Hesse-Cassel, one of the small independent German states. He tried to find work with the local carpenters and blacksmiths, but he was always recognized and driven off with threats and curses. He soon became a tramp and a vagabond, cast out by everyone. Suddenly, when he was at his wits' end, he was found by a prince, His Highness Prince Karl, the Count of Hesse-Cassel himself. Prince Karl was a kindly man in his fifties who had taken up mechanics as a hobby and was now obsessed by the idea of perpetual motion. He had followed Orffyreus's progress with interest and was delighted when he heard that Orffyreus was seeking work in his own state. For some time he had had scouts out looking for the restless inventor, and for Orffyreus it must have seemed like a dream come true when they found him and took him to the Count's castle.

Orffyreus explained his theories to the Count and drew him diagrams of the amazing wheels. The Count was obviously very impressed, for he offered to provide whatever Orffyreus needed to prove to the world that he really could build a machine that needed no fuel to drive it. The Count also made him a town councillor and gave him his own suite of rooms in the castle, a turn of events that brought back all Orffyreus's vitality and enthusiasm. He built his fourth and largest wheel in one of the empty rooms of the castle. The wheel was put on exhibition there and remained on show for several months. It was a popular sight and many important and well-qualified people travelled miles to see it. All were satisfied that the machine was not a fraud and the rumour spread through Europe that at long last the secret of perpetual motion had been found.

Finally the Count invited two distinguished scientists to come and give their opinion of the machine. The two experts, Baron Fischer and Professor Willem s'Gravesande (a close friend of Sir Isaac Newton), made no secret of their reasons for going to see Orffyreus's wheel. They called him 'a rascally pretender and an unscrupulous leech' and made no bones about the fun they would have in proving it. Orffyreus became surly and quarrelsome as soon as they arrived, for he realized immediately that they were out to discredit him. Prince Karl tried to reassure him, but Orffyreus insisted that although he would show the scientists the wheel, he would on no account allow them to see the internal workings until the invention 'had been paid for'.

The scientists were taken to the workroom, which was built like a prison with walls four feet thick, no windows and only one door. In the middle of the bare and gloomy chamber stood the last 'wheel of eternity'. It was twelve feet across and about two feet thick and also had a covering of canvas to prevent the inside workings from being seen. It was suspended above the floor with its thin axle pivoting through uprights of light wood. At the top of these two uprights there were wooden cross-pieces from which long pendulums hung. Orffyreus looked on sneeringly while the experts minutely examined the outside of the structure. Finding no hidden wires or suspicious-looking ropes, they asked the inventor to make the machine work for them. Orffyreus reached forward and gave the wheel a gentle push and it slowly began to revolve, gradually accelerating until it settled down to a speed of twenty-six revolutions per minute. After watching for some time the two observers asked Orffyreus to stop the wheel, which he did simply by stretching out his hand and holding the wheel firmly.

The Baron and the Professor were certainly impressed, but this was only the beginning of their investigation. The rest of that day and most of the next they spent stripping down all the outside parts of the machine, tapping and testing until they were certain that no trickery was involved. Finally they asked to see the machine working in a completely different room. The wheel was moved and worked perfectly. As the investigations wore on the experts became more and more bewildered, while Orffyreus became very bad-tempered and hostile. On the third day the Professor and the Baron suggested that the room should be sealed, leaving the wheel working away inside it. Sometime in the future, perhaps in a week or a couple of months, they would return and see if the wheel were still revolving. Orffyreus was still suspicious but he agreed. It seemed a small price to pay to get rid of the two men whom he had come to despise.

On 12 November 1717 the machine was locked away and the room sealed with the scientists' own seals.

Eight weeks later, on 4 January 1718, Baron Fischer and Professor s'Gravesande returned and asked for the room to be reopened. The seals were carefully examined, found to be intact, and sure enough, when the door was pushed open, the wheel was whirring and grinding as smoothly and happily as ever. Orffyreus was delighted to see the dismay that was clearly written on the faces of the men who had hoped to catch him out! But his happiness quickly disappeared when they told him that they didn't understand how the machine worked and asked him to explain it. 'You will understand how it works when it is paid for!' he yelled. 'And I will not take less than 20,000 English sovereigns!' The experts were staggered by the great sum the inventor expected for his secret, but they agreed that it was certainly no ordinary secret and the Professor promised to write to his friend Sir Isaac Newton about it.

After the men left the room Orffyreus sank into a brooding silence, and the longer he thought, the more he became convinced that the scientists were out to steal his secret. An unpopular and misunderstood outcast all his life, the young inventor found it impossible to believe that anyone would ever pay him his rightful dues. Karl tried to persuade him that this was not so and that in a very short time he would be wealthy and famous – but Orffyreus would not listen. Later that night a fearful crashing sound came from the workroom. In a fit of passion Orffyreus was smashing his creation to pieces. The Count and the scientists rushed to the chamber and found that all that was left of the inventor and his wheel were angry words daubed on the wall and a heap of unrecognizable splinters. It was said that Orffyreus had stormed off into the woods to take up the wild nomadic life he had lived before. There were odd rumours that Orffyreus was building another wheel so that all the experts, who were now convinced that he was not a fraud, could be invited to see it. Yet there are no records of another wheel or perpetual-motion machine of any kind being exhibited anywhere. All we know is that Orffyreus died in 1745, taking his fascinating secret to the grave with him.

What possible mechanism could have been hidden inside that wheel? What was the secret lurking behind a thin layer of linen which was so very nearly revealed to the world? Orffyreus was certainly deranged, possibly quite mad, but he could easily have been a brilliant inventor, or, on the other hand, a very clever confidence trickster! Many well-qualified people of the time were prepared to swear he was genuine, yet if this was so, why did he wait until he was so near to acclaim before disappearing? Also, if his wheel was so simple to construct, it is difficult to believe that no one else discovered it. Still, perhaps if Orffyreus revealed his secret today, we would have no further need for atomic power!

13 The Russian princess: alive or dead?

During the Russian Revolution in 1917 when the Communists succeeded in overthrowing the Czarist regime, Czar Nicholas II, the ruling monarch, and his entire family were captured and held prisoner in a house in Ekaterinburg. Although the Czar had abdicated in 1917 and been kept under heavy guard ever since, the Communists were still concerned about his future as they feared that while he was allowed to stay alive a counter-revolution might be planned by his followers. Finally on 16 July 1918 the Ekaterinburg soviet finally called for the execution of the entire Romanov family. This meant not only the Czar, his wife and their son and heir Alexei Nicholaievitch, but also their four lovely daughters – Tatiana, Olga, Maria and Anastasia – plus three servants and the Czar's personal physician, Dr Eugene Botkin. On that fateful day the prisoners were awakened shortly before midnight and herded into a cellar by several soldiers. The local commissar then arrived and read aloud a death warrant to the sleepy and bewildered family.

Before any of them had time to understand what was happening, the commissar drew his revolver and shot the Czar through the head. The soldiers at once joined in the assassination by spraying bullets into all the prisoners in the cellar. They did not stop firing until they were satisfied that their victims were quite dead. Any slight movement or moan caused another shot to be fired. Early the following morning the bodies were taken to a nearby mining village where they were buried in a pit and covered with sulphuric acid in order to make them charred and unrecognizable. This dreadful massacre was the sad finale to the proud Romanov dynasty which had ruled Russia for more than 300 years. Yet it was only the beginning of the curious legends which were to keep the Romanov name alive! It began with rumours, which gradually became more widespread, that one of the members of the family had made a miraculous escape. At first it was whispered to be the Romanov heir Alexei, then later one of his sisters – Tatiana or Anastasia. Eventually the rumour faded away since no Russian prince or princess had come forward to confirm it.

One day in 1920, however, a policeman in Berlin was crossing a bridge spanning the Landwehr Canal when he saw a woman poised on the parapet. Although he called out to her, she launched herself forward and dropped into the icy-cold water. The brave policeman immediately jumped in after her and dragged her unconscious body from the canal. She was taken to a nearby hospital and revived and then sent on to the Dalldorf Sanatorium where she was kept for the next two years. The physician who admitted her judged her age to be about twenty and found her to be suffering from loss of memory, probably brought on by shock. One of the patients at Dalldorf, Klara Peuthert, immediately recognized the frail young girl and announced that she was undoubtedly the Czar's second daughter, Tatiana. She told this amazing piece of news to Baron Arthur van Kleist, whom she thought could still contact people who knew the Czar's daughter very well. He contacted the late Empress's lady-in-waiting, a woman called Baroness Buxhoevan, and together they went to the sanatorium to see the young patient. The Baroness knew at once that this could not be Tatiana, for she was the tallest of the Czar's daughters, whereas this girl was quite short. Surely it must be the youngest daughter, Anastasia!

The young woman, who finally gave her name as Mrs Anna Tchaikovsky, was persuaded to tell who she was and how she came to be in Berlin. The story she told was to cause a sensation! She confirmed that her name had been Anastasia and that on that dreadful night of July 16th she had indeed been led into a dark cellar with the rest of her family and shot. However, one of the Russian soldiers assigned to dispose of the corpses the following morning found her badly wounded but still alive. After the horror of the previous night he just could not bear to kill her and felt it was worth becoming a deserter if he could save her from death. The soldier, Alexander Tchaikovsky, and his brother Sergei managed to hide Anastasia's broken body from the rest of the soldiers and concealed her in another part of the house while they waited for a convenient time to make their escape. The following night while the house was sleeping they crept away with Anastasia to a nearby farmhouse. There they tended her wounds, dressed her as a peasant and made their way to the Romanian border in a horse and cart. No one bothered to search for the deserting soldiers since food was desperately short at that time and two fewer mouths to feed couldn't be a bad thing. In any case many soldiers, sick of the bloodshed and hard times of this terrible revolution, were deserting and returning to their homes to discover the fate of their families and possessions.

The memory of the journey was a nightmare: 1,500 miles of rough roads and rickety carts, cold weather and not enough to eat. The pain of her wounds was always with Anastasia, and the memory of that night in the cellar when her entire family was wiped out was something she could never put out of her thoughts. The one good thing was the valuable emeralds that the brothers had found sewn into her clothing. The Czarina, hoping that one day the family might escape or be released, had sewn bits of her jewellery into her daughters' dresses as an insurance against starvation. Certainly the sale of the emeralds now helped Anastasia and the Tchaikovsky brothers to stay alive, and by the middle of winter they had reached Bucharest in safety. There Anastasia gratefully married her rescuer, Alexander, and together with his brother Sergei they lived quietly in Bucharest, telling no one of their secret. Soon afterwards Anastasia gave birth to a son and for a short time her life became almost bearable again. However, shortly after the birth, Anastasia's husband was found shot dead in the street. The baby was immediately taken from its mother and put into an orphanage. Apparently the Communist leader, Trotsky, had learned of Anastasia's escape and had finally traced the fugitives to Bucharest, where he set a trap for them.

The young widow and her brother-in-law snatched up a few possessions and fled. They had heard that there were many Russian fugitives in Berlin and decided to make their way there. They crossed the German border safely and when they reached Berlin took rooms in a cheap hotel. Sergei, although fond of Anastasia, was terrified of being traced and then assassinated and decided that he could no longer risk his own life by protecting the Russian princess. Once Anastasia was asleep he left the hotel and was never seen again. Shortly afterwards the girl awoke and found that he had taken his things and left. This was the last straw for Anastasia. Everyone she had been close to since birth had been snatched away from her – her family, her husband and her child. The violence she had seen in the last two years came crowding in on her. She wandered the streets of the city aimlessly until she came to the bridge over the canal. It seemed a very easy way to escape from her nightmare. After that she remembered nothing until she awoke in the sanatorium.

The full story was released to the world and caused a great deal of speculation. It seemed a credible story, but why had not Anastasia declared before now that she was the Grand Duchess? The Russian refugees in Berlin seemed to be split into two camps, those who thought she was genuine and gave her a place in their Russian colony, and the others who thought she was a fake! Such bitterness arose between the two factions that it was decided Anastasia's true identity must be established as soon as possible. Various people were brought to confront her but the most dramatic occasion was when one of the royal nannies was brought forward. Her name was Sascha and she had attended the Grand Duchess Anastasia for several years in St Petersburg. In spite of the crowds of women in the room at the time, Sascha rushed up to Mrs Tchaikovsky and fell on her knees before her. Mrs Tchaikovsky recognized her in turn and called her 'Zhura', a pet name for the nanny that had been used only by Anastasia as a very small child. There was certainly no doubt in the nurse's mind that this was indeed the Grand Duchess.

Yet other witnesses were not so definite. Anastasia's godmother, Princess Irene, was brought from Romania to meet the controversial young woman, although she had last seen Anastasia ten years previously. Anna Tchaikovsky's withdrawn and hostile personality seemed totally alien to that of the warm-hearted, outgoing Anastasia that she remembered. Yet the girl's features and bearing were undoubtedly the same. Although she could not be sure it was Anastasia, she certainly couldn't say that it was someone else! The Crown Princess Cecilie of Germany was also introduced to Mrs Tchaikovsky and could not definitely decide one way or the other. Although the girl looked very like the Czar and resembled Anastasia in every way, it was her obstinate silence and total lack of warmth which also made the Princess unsure of her. Other people firmly denied the existence of Anastasia. One of the royal children's tutors, for instance, was quite convinced that this was not the girl he had taught.

Finally the Danish ambassador was sent to look into the puzzle by Anastasia's Aunt Olga. Although he had never met the Czar's youngest daughter, he was a brilliant scholar and found the problem of Mrs Tchaikovsky's identity a great challenge. Ambassador Zahle scrutinized Mrs Tchaikovsky very carefully and compared her physical characteristics with those of the Grand Duchess. The young widow resembled the photos of the Duchess in the royal family album very closely; not only that, but she bore specific identity marks as well. One finger of her left hand was badly maimed just as Anastasia's had been when she had it slammed in a car door. (The rest of the family had forgotten this accident until Anna Tchaikovsky mentioned it herself.) There was a scar on her right shoulder where Anastasia had had a large wart removed in infancy, and her feet were badly deformed by bunions, just as Anastasia's had been. She was also found to be suffering from severe tuberculosis of the bone, a disease that was common to several members of the Romanov family.

On the other hand, facts came to light which were to cast doubts on her claim. The most serious of these was her apparent inability to speak Russian, English and French, subjects in which she had been well tutored as a child. The only language she appeared to speak fluently was German, a language she should never even have heard before. Obviously it is possible to forget subjects learned in childhood, but never to suddenly remember a language you have never even learned! No trace was ever found in Germany or Romania of her husband's brother Sergei Tchaikovsky, and although orphanages were apparently searched in Bucharest no child that could have been Anna Tchaikovsky's was ever discovered.

Suddenly, in 1927, a private detective came forward with information which shed completely new light on the mystery. He happened to know that a Polish peasant girl had disappeared from her Berlin apartment on 15 February 1920. The girl, whose name was Franziska Senanzkovsky, also had a family history of bone tuberculosis, and her medical records showed that she had some sort of foot deformity and had had a birthmark removed from her left shoulder (though Anastasia's had been on the right shoulder). The detective also produced the daughter of Franziska's landlady who was prepared to swear that Mrs Tchaikovsky and her mother's missing tenant were one and the same. Yet when Franziska's own brother was produced, he admitted that Anna bore a certain resemblance to his sister but was not at all convinced that she was Franziska. This confused the issue even more. With all the different views and theories of the people who had known either Anastasia or the Polish peasant girl, not one had a shred of concrete evidence to prove that Anna was either one person or the other!

Mrs Tchaikovsky finally went to court in an attempt to establish her identity, for she told Ambassador Zahle that the Czar had deposited twenty million roubles (seven million dollars) for each of his daughters in an English bank. If Anna could prove that she was the sole-surviving Russian princess she would, of course, be entitled to four times that amount, not to mention the money the Czar had left for his son! If Mrs Tchaikovsky were discredited, however, the money would go to the remaining exiled Romanovs and the Hesse-Darmstadt family in Germany, most of whom had done their best to prove that Anna was an imposter.

In 1933 the Berlin Civil Court ignored Mrs Tchaikovsky and gave the remaining claimants a document of inheritance to the Romanov fortune. This marked the beginning of a drawn-out legal battle that has raged for the last fifty years while witnesses who might have helped have died, and documents and evidence have been destroyed or lost. This unfortunate woman spent her entire adult life claiming to be Anastasia, Grand Duchess of Imperial Russia. Is she or isn't she? Unless new evidence comes to light we shall never know, for the facts have become worn and distorted by time. One thing is certain, however: the whereabouts of the millions of roubles the Czar was said to have bequeathed to his son and daughters has never been discovered. If Mrs Tchaikovsky knew that her half-a-century fight for recognition could not eventually bring her financial gain, why on earth did she bother?

14 The strange curse of the Lost Dutchman's Mine

Somewhere in a remote canyon in the Superstition Mountains of Arizona lies the fabulous and long-sought 'Lost Dutchman's Mine'. The gold mine was first shown to white men by friendly Apache Indians long before the Indians learned of the white man's greed for gold. Soon afterwards rumours of the large deposits of gold in this newly discovered mine reached Mexico and many expeditions were made across the 250 miles to the mine in the Superstition Mountains. The explorers returned weighed down with sacks of the gold and told how easy it had been, as the gold could easily be dug out by the spadeful. In 1890 it was said that the mine belonged to a man called Don Miguel Peralta whose family had been given it in 1748 by King Ferdinand VI of Spain, along with 3,750 square miles of what is now the middle of the State of Arizona. No one called Don Miguel Peralta ever came forward, and in 1895 a man named James Addison was convicted of forging documents giving a non-existent Land Grant to an equally non-existent Don Miguel Peralta.

Yet sometime in 1871 the elusive Don Miguel Peralta had apparently taken two men called Weiser and Waltz to the mysterious mine and given them an old map which quite clearly marked the exact location of the gold. According to their story the mine had been worked for many years by Don Miguel and his family, who had a heavy bodyguard to fight off the no longer friendly Apaches. In spite of this bodyguard the Indians eventually managed to kill most of Don Miguel's party in a three-day pitched battle which took place in 1864, and only a few survivors, including Don Miguel himself, escaped to Mexico. Don Miguel, now penniless and depressed, decided to settle in a small town called Arizpe. One day he became involved in a street fight and the two Americans, Weiser and Waltz, rescued him from a beating. In a burst of gratitude he told them all about his wonderful mine and said that if the two new-found friends would agree to go back to the mine with him, he would give them a half share of the gold. Their mission was apparently successful and $60,000 worth of gold was brought back. On their return, however, Don Miguel decided that he needed all this batch of gold himself, but in return he gave the two Americans the map and sole rights to the gold in the mine, instead of their promised half-share – a much better deal for the Americans!

Whether their story was true or whether the Americans had in fact stolen or even killed for the precious map we shall never know, but there is no doubt that Weiser and Waltz knew the way to the mine. They returned together to the

Superstition Mountains in 1879, always moving under cover of darkness and with great stealth. They set up their camp and then both went off to dig in different places. When Waltz made his way back to the camp later that day he found that Weiser had disappeared, leaving behind him clothing drenched in blood and several Indian arrows. Waltz was terrified and, with his mind full of scalpings and hideous Apache tortures, he fled, taking with him as much of the gold as he could carry. He settled in a town called Phoenix in Arizona and lived there very quietly until 1891.

Meanwhile Weiser, a badly wounded prisoner of the Apaches, had somehow managed to escape and make his way to the house of Doctor John Walker. His wounds were so severe, however, that he died of them, after handing his map over to the doctor. Dr Walker, for reasons of his own, made no attempt to go to the mine, and on his own death in 1890 the map mysteriously vanished, leaving Waltz as the only person who knew the location of the mine.

Yet in 1880 two unknown young men rode into the town of Pinal, their saddlebags bursting with large gold nuggets which they said had come from a mine in the Superstition Mountains. On their way back to the canyon for a return visit they mysteriously disappeared. A rescue party sent out ten days later found them strung up on a tree with their clothes removed and shot through the head. It looked like a typical Apache killing except that the bullets came from a US Army gun! The murderer was never discovered.

After this, rumours of a fabulously rich gold mine had spread through Arizona like wildfire and suddenly many men claimed to know where it was. So in 1882 the Apaches decided to take a hand. They brought a party of their squaws to fill the mine in. There are also stories of an earthquake in the canyon around that time which must have confused the location even more. In spite of all these efforts, Jacob Waltz left Phoenix in 1890 and returned with a sackful of gold worth $1,500. He died a short time later after giving the neighbours around his death bed a description of the mine and instructions for finding it. He said that it was a funnel-shaped pit situated in rough country and contained large gold nuggets that just fell out when you tapped them with a hammer. He said that someone, presumably Don Miguel's father, had cut a tunnel through the hillside into the bottom of the pit to make it easier to take out large amounts of gold. His neighbours searched and searched but never did find it, and because they thought that Waltz was Dutch, the mine became known as the 'Lost Dutchman's Mine'.

Ever since Waltz's death hundreds of men have searched for the lost mine and its fabulous wealth. At least twenty of them have been murdered by unknown assailants, though as far as we know no one has seen the Dutchman's Mine since 1890 (or if they have, they didn't live to tell the tale). A typical killing was that of Adolph Ruth, who claimed that he was off to make a search with a map he had been given by a relative of the Peralta family. When he was eventually found he had been shot twice in the forehead and then beheaded.

Who commits these bizarre murders? Is there really someone who knows where the mine is and is guarding it for reasons of his own? Is there even a gold mine at all? If the story is true, why should Don Miguel Peralta have handed over such fabulous wealth to two comparative strangers after defending the mine against hordes of Apaches for so many years? We will never know the answers to most of these questions, but we do know that there really was a mine. In an area near 'Weaver's Needle', a landmark mentioned in every account, there are clear signs that many people, probably Mexicans, worked there. There are deeply worn trails, sawn-off tree stumps, the trunks of which were probably used as pit-props, piles of Mexican sandals, and in the mountains themselves the bones of hundreds of mules which were probably killed and eaten by the Apaches after the massacre of Don Miguel's miners.

The question remains, will the mine ever be found again? And if so, will it confirm or refute the stories and legends written about it? As man's greed for gold seems to have caused so many fatal accidents, perhaps it would be better if the mine stayed lost for ever!